In High Places

In High Places

DOUGAL HASTON

CANONGATE

First published in 1972 by Cassell & Company Ltd.

This edition published in 1997 by
Canongate Books Ltd, 14 High Street, Edinburgh

ISBN 0 86241 700 3

Printed and bound in Finland by WSOY

Contents

Introduction

Dougal Haston always brought the best out in the people who climbed with him; certainly it was always, for me, a very demanding and testing time. Once again and, as it turned out, for the last time, his determination and cool logic showed itself on the huge 7,000-foot South Face of Mount McKinley in April 1976 when a ferocious storm had us pinned down for two nights, and we were only 2,000 feet up the face. On the third morning, with spindrift blowing into our open bivouac and with 5,000 feet still to go, I shouted above the storm to Dougal, 'Well, what do you reckon about our chances?'

That hard Scotsman looked me in the eye and asked, 'Well, have you got frostbite?'

'No,' I replied.

He shrugged, letting me know that we go on until we do and hopefully get there before that happens.

It did not happen and after four more very cold and miserable bivouacs we climbed onto the summit, having made the first alpine-style ascent of a new route on the mountain. I have always remembered the 'Dougal Dictum' that encapsulated the criteria Dougal applied to climbing in high places.

Dougal was born Duncan MacSporan Haston at Currie, Midlothian, Scotland in 1940. On the 17th January 1977 he died above the Swiss village of Leysin below a minor peak called Riondaz. With his death, Britain lost one of the finest mountaineers to have come from these Isles.

Dougal's climbing was a classic concentric progression, first climbing locally with schoolboy friends and then ever-widening circles encompassing local crag, Highland winter gully and summer rock face. In 1959 he visited the Alps for the first time and during the next four years he climbed some of the great classics and the harder new routes in the Dolomites. His attention then turned to the Eiger North Face and after three attempts he made the second British ascent in 1963. This climb brought him national recognition and in 1966 he was acclaimed internationally for his central part in climbing the Eiger direct. The following year he consolidated his winter climbing with a bold winter ascent up the Matterhorn North Face, and all this before the drop pick ice axe had been invented. In 1968 he joined a strong British team that just failed to climb Cerro Torre in wild Patagonia.

On his first visit to the Himalaya in 1970 he succeeded in reaching the summit of Annapurna via the horrendous South Face. The following year he was back to try the South-west Face of Everest – the highest of all the faces. He did not reach the summit but he did put in an incredible effort on that ill-fated international expedition. He came away with his reputation untarnished and, in fact, enhanced.

Dougal was back on Everest the following year on Chris Bonington's first expedition. It was unsuccessful in climbing the South-west Face but Dougal again was at the high point and I was with him on that occasion when we took the decision to abandon the attempt on the 14th of November. We had not only come too late but we also realised that we had gone the wrong way. We had to wait three years before Everest became available to us and, in the meantime, Dougal was making winter ascents in the Alps and was also on the first ascent of Changabang in the Garwhal Himal with Chris Bonington, Mark Boysen, Balwant Sandhu, Tashi Chewang and myself.

Chris again booked Everest, this time in the autumn of 1975. His planning was implemented to perfection and he had a very strong team that walked in a month earlier and that aimed to climb the left-hand gully of the rockband. This was achieved by Nick Estcourt and Paul Braithwaite. Dougal and I established Camp VI above the rockband and pushed out fixed rope across the upper snowfield on the first day. On the second – the 24th September – we reached the top of the face and climbed the final part of the original route to the summit of Everest. That night was spent in an unplanned bivouac by the south summit at 28,700 feet without sleeping bags and without oxygen. We survived without frostbite and managed to get ourselves down to the western coomb the following day. Those three days above the rockband were the finest days one could ever hope to have on a mountain. It was not only the place but the person I was with. I always felt privileged in Dougal's company and certainly on the South-west Face of Everest it became obvious why. He was very much like a sherpa – reticent, self-contained, economical in word and deed. He never wasted a step yet took every pitch that came his way; he never faltered. His physical and moral strength transmitted itself to me, giving me the confidence to concentrate on taking that next step in a place where every step gets more difficult.

The following spring Dougal and I made our way up the South Face of Mount McKinley. Dougal took the rest of the year off to write his novel, *Calculated Risk*. The irony of the ski-ing incident described in the book, when the hero Jack McDonald out-runs a powder snow avalanche on La Riondaz, is matched against the incident in real life in which Dougal perished. Only a few days after passing over his hand-written manuscript, he himself went out to ski the same couloir. The warnings were up not to ski above the town of Leysin that day as there was so much powder lying on the mountains. To ski down La Riondaz couloir in those conditions was something that Dougal had long planned to do. He was obviously aware of the dangers as he set off. He skied down the couloir but triggered off an avalanche which overwhelmed him. He was found the following day buried under a few feet of snow.

His historic climbing achievements only hint at the man himself. There are revelations of his character in this book, *In High Places*. It is succinctly written without superfluous padding, jarring like rap at times, taking the reader up his climbs – ever longer, ever harder, ever higher. Along the way we have glimpses of his metaphysical development, as he passed from rebellion into a period of spiritual confusion until, finally, he was beginning to show an awareness and acceptance of what is. Although, having said that, he had an unusual if not paranoid obsession with armchair critics coming 'out of their holes' to annoy him. Certainly, towards the end of his life and beyond the scope of this book, he did seem more tranquil; perhaps that was to do with the merciless passage of time as with all of us.

So, in this book, the reader will trace the development of the climber and the man, but mostly the climber. For although he climbs 'to find out more about himself' he keeps most of his discoveries to himself and his life beyond climbing is hardly dealt with at all; the fact that he married is given one sentence. He was not sentimental but he was a climber and that is what this book is about.

The first two pages set the scene and develop a theme that runs through the book – how he was able to bend his will to maintain upward progress through the most adverse conditions when he was fully convinced of the logic of the route. In fact, he never faltered, never backed down; took every pitch on a climb that came his way. He was helped in this by an ability to acclimatise quickly and with vast reserves of strength. He was a supreme athlete – an aristocrat amongst the rest. He was, by nature, physically suited to climbing and he did have a strong competitive streak as is revealed in his early years when competing with Sassenachs for plumb climbs in Glencoe and on the Ben. His natural aptitude for climbing would have come to nought had he not served a very long and hard apprenticeship – 'getting out of difficult situations successfully by the strength of our own ability' – in Scotland, the Dolomites and the Alps, which helped him accumulate a store of knowledge to survive situations on the great faces of Annapurna and Everest.

Doug Scott
March, 1997

A View from Camp VI

Two months out and still only at twenty-four. Is it despair? Do you really worry if you get up or not? The mind is often so blank. Getting up doing the same monotonous tasks. Is this the blinding up unknown walls in the remoter parts of the world, that you have chosen above all other things? Often it seems like a routine job. Up, out, work, back to bed. Instead of earning a wage you are earning mountain experience. Pessimism, pessimism, it so easily creeps in. Such a huge and wild situation is all too conducive to self-doubt. Self-doubt magnified beyond all proportion can drive you completely from the mountain. It is the reasonable elimination of this doubt that makes you a better climber. Self-doubt along with fear is necessary. But can you control them both? This is where climbing is that much more than just pitting body against mountain. In many ways it seems unreasonable. But what could be more reasonable than finding out about yourself? In many ways a large expedition is a great test of this. It is not only the ability to assimilate the vagaries and normalities in the minds of others. It is the ability to control them in your own. Working against a big objective brings much despair. Progress can be so small. Certain functions such as load carrying can be so unrewarding. I know they are satisfying in relation to eventual success, but they are so unsatisfying in themselves. There are so many tasks in a big expedition. Eventually there exists an almost primitive hierarchy. It is the survival of the fittest. The sick have no function. In terms of health it is a gradual wastage process. From the high hopes and ideals at the start you eventually approach a weary climax. We were down as a team after our first summit rebuff. As a unit we were about forty per cent efficient. Hammering defeat was close and looking likelier

with every gust of wind and blast of spindrift. It's a strange feeling
to be at the top of a toppling pyramid. . . .

The product of perhaps five minutes' thought at Camp VI on
the South Face of Annapurna. A few moments of philosophical
pessimism. Strange though it may seem, I was happy.

Camp VI as always, breeze big wind rocked. Why does it stay on?
Bodies shifting uncomfortable in the night. Troubled thoughts with
summit dreams mixed. Breath exhaled into rime and frost to melt
into wet with the morning stove. Boots on feet in frozen sleeping-bag
as they have been for the last seven nights. Morning; moving, and
up because there can be no down. The mind is aware of only one
choice. The will commands, weakened though the body may be.
It is Don who is there. We are clothed alike. We have the same
objective. But in the mind, what a difference: the practical and the
philosophical! He has a job to do and is doing it. I have a way of life
to live and am living it. Onward, outward, creeping on jumars and
rimed ropes. It is cold: a cold cold colder than the coldest cold of our
benumbed experience. Dachstein-mitted hands freeze in jumar
clutch. Even an additional pair doesn't help too much. Toes are
where? Freezing in four boot layers. We move on. Out of the gully
and desperate cold into vague sun. Sun as hot as sun can be at
26,000 feet. Covered suddenly by a wild burst of spindrift. Uncovered
noses sharply freezing. A ridge ahead, an icy buttress and blue sky.
Still the upward movement. Solo bodies a hundred feet apart.
Thoughts not too dissimilar for once. Concentration precluding
mental wandering. Then there was one body and the blue sky.
Then the two meet again against the sky with the rock and snow
beneath. It's all over. But where did it all begin?

CHAPTER ONE

Rock Bottom

Where did it all begin? Sometimes I don't really think I can trace a beginning. Many people hill-walk in Scotland. I certainly did from the age of six onwards. Also being born in the country, in a small village called Currie six miles from Edinburgh, gave a child an interest in the hills. However, I shall search my mind for shadowy traces of a love of rock.

One early teenage day in 1954 Jim Moriarty—a schoolfriend of the same age, known as Eley—and I were walking along a disused railway track. We were bored. The usual object of the walk was to throw stones at cats, climb a few trees or maybe go into the privately owned woods to annoy the gamekeepers, who could never run as fast as we could. Yet it seemed as if we had done it all before. It was still daylight so we couldn't go hunt the girls.

I was throwing an idle stone in the Water of Leith, the local river, when Eley said, 'Let's climb this wall.' The wall being a mossy conglomeration of stones which was holding up a near-by embankment. 'All right,' said I, and we launched into what could have been the start of a climbing career. We seemed to enjoy it.

Soon after, at the age of fourteen, I fell into the capable and altruistic hands of the local youth club leader, Alick Buchanan Smith. His was the introduction to the bigger hills of Scotland. These are relatively small, mostly around 3,000 feet, and called 'Munros'. At this stage we didn't do any rock climbing. Long plods over grassy slopes and ridges gave fitness and something more. A glimmering of aesthetic appreciation began to show in the mind of a working-class fourteen-year-old. Sunrises, sunsets; the beauty of cloud; a snowy windblown day being something more than for making snowballs.

In my formal education these were alien things: sports were the team sweat of football and the sudden fierce competition of track

3

athletics. Gradually the new interest began to give more. I still combined the three but the hill-walking holidays began to be looked forward to.

Then at fourteen came the most significant event, the first rock climb. It seemed to come as a reward for staying hard on the heels of the leader for many a long walk. Alick was no great rock climber, but a friend had turned up in the camp who had led up to difficult standard. There were two of us to go, Jim Stenhouse and myself. Our happy feelings worked in two directions. One which showed the predominately banal state of our minds at that time, the other which held a piece of hope for a future. The first was that we were going and others weren't. Oneupmanship. Second was the chance to approach the almost magical rock faces. To our minds at that time anything over a hundred feet high was an awesome thing. No one in Currie had ever gone climbing. It was a sport for well-off people, and Currie was certainly not that kind of area.

Consequently rock climbing was dismissed as eccentric and mad—the normal working man's interpretation of the foibles of one who doesn't toil for a living. Cliffs were just part of the Lord's world, and if they were to be tampered with it had to be for some practical purpose like quarrying. Certainly not to be swarmed over for pleasure. Our fourteen-year-old minds were grappling with this kind of conditioning. But we were full of comic and adventure-book stories where the hero clambers up a thousand-foot overhang and wipes out the enemy garrison at the top. Also, the last thing we could do would be to chicken out. This would have been ridicule at the hands of the others. Nothing was worse at that age. We went.

The climb? Curved ridge on Buachaille Etive Mor in Glencoe. Vague memories of rock scenery that made our hearts beat. No technique but it's the easiest route on the mountain. Athletic youth made up for lack of skill. Vertical walls all around.

'A question, sir . . . . People surely can't go up there?'

'There are quite standard ways and lots of people climb them.'

Deflation of our egos. We were only normal after all. These people must be superhuman.

The interest remained though. On to high school and the discovery of a library that had climbing books. My parents made me go to the church every Sunday, but *Nanga Parbat Pilgrimage* by Hermann Buhl, an autobiography by the foremost Austrian climber in the years after the war, was studied much more than the Bible—or school text books, for that matter. It seemed another world but we kept on dreaming and practising on our railway walls. There was no money. Therefore no equipment. Six-inch nails for pitons and clothesline for rope. Very early discoveries as to the inadequacy of both. Stunning twenty-foot leaps into the Water of Leith. This was by no means like falling off sea cliffs like the Calanques of later years. Two paper-mills and a tannery poured their refuse into it. One emerged scraped and stinking to limp home like a leper. No sympathy there however. Money was tight and clothes precious, and severe scoldings made our disgrace complete.

We also learnt early lessons about 'objective dangers'—the climber's phrase for threats over which he has no control, such as stonefall, crevasses or collapsing séracs. There was one traverse right above the river. You'd be groping along it when a crowd of kids would appear and throw stones. By the time you dropped off and chased them they were gone, and if confronted face to face the next day they always had a brother or cousin bigger than you. But on cooling down and drying out a re-reading of Hermann Buhl would make it all seem worth while. This was our Karwendel and Kaisergebirge—the classic training-grounds of Austrian climbers. I would retire for long periods to my room. Parents were happy: great thoughts of Higher Leaving Certificate and an educated son. But the only mathematical problem the son was attending to was the rate of stonefall on an ascent of the North Face of the Eiger.

The Way Up

Mountains have always exerted a strange influence on man. Grim and inaccessible, dwelling-places of gods and spirits, they have always had an aura of the unknown and the mysterious. Mountain exploration is a relatively recent thing, and for many the old thoughts linger on. Perhaps that's why mountaineers are thought to be oddities.

But is it so odd to want a little adventure, to do a little exploration, to be a little bit of an individual in the over-organized mess? Even the most modest mountaineer achieves something when he takes his feet off the ground and launches upward. He is doing something on his own. Mountaineering has developed into an activity with rules and ethical codes, but these are not restrictive, merely a safety precaution.

To read easily about climbers and climbing, it is necessary to have some knowledge of the basic techniques and equipment. There are many strange misconceptions floating around.

'How do you get the rope up there in the first place so you can climb it?'

'You must need strong arms to throw up the grapnels.'

'I remember when we used to climb the ropes in the gym at school. I could only manage it a few times; how the hell you do it for thousands of feet beats me!'

These are the people with fixed ideas about the use of the rope. It's not surprising: in adventure stories—and at least one popular author has a thing about climbers—its always thrown up or fired from a gun, and then the intrepid climber tackles a hundred feet or so hand over hand, pausing only to grit his teeth and bang a few metal spikes into the rock with his bare fists. In real life, unfortunately, we climbers can do neither, but then we do not even qualify as sportsmen. 'Climbing is a pastime, not a sport.' Poor outcasts!

To many people climbing has different meanings and levels, but with its rules, systems and ethical codes it is no more irrational than hitting a ball around a court or field, driving a car faster than anyone else, or trying to knock hell out of someone's head.

An average cliff to a non-climber is a lump of rock, and that's about all. There are a few people whose professional eyes might look for something more—the artist its form; the geologist its structure; the botanist the plant-life upon it. To the climber, however, it's a whole complex little world. How many routes? What standard? Any possibility of anything new? Routes, standard, novelty—what is he talking about.

Let's take a practical example. Two climbers come to an unexplored cliff roughly two hundred feet high and decide they want to climb it. They'll look at the rock and try to figure out a continuous route or 'line' by which they will be able to climb straight up. One of them will be carrying a rope, around 150 feet long. This is usually made out of nylon and between 9 and 11 millimetres in diameter. The advantages of nylon ropes are that they are strong and light and can take a lot of punishment. It has to be light so as not to affect the climber's balance when he is moving, and also

strong enough to hold a fall. It is usually coiled up fairly tightly so
that it can be slung round the shoulders and hang down to around
the waist. A more loosely coiled rope could catch the climber's legs
when he walks.

As well as the long rope one of the pair would probably be carrying
some 'slings' or short loops of single-thickness 7–9-millimetre rope
with oval metal snaplinks, called carabiners, attached. The first
man will wrap the rope once or twice round his waist and fasten it
off with a knot that won't come undone—say a bowline—then pass
the remainder of the rope through his hands, making sure there are
no kinks or knots, until he comes to the other end. This end he hands
to the second man, who ties on in the same fashion as the first.
Before the leader sets off, the second man will 'belay', attach himself
to the rock so that he can't be pulled off if the leader falls. Here
he would take a loop in the rope, or one of his slings, and put it round
a projecting piece of solid rock, tying himself in as close as possible.
Then he puts the part of the rope closest to the leader round his
waist, and lets it out gently as the first man starts to climb. It's very
important that he keeps the rope running smoothly and easily; on
difficult ground the slightest tug could pull the leader off. As the
first man starts up the face he looks for holds, projections and rock
formations on which he can put his hands and feet. He doesn't just
find something for his hands and muscle up with scrabbling feet.
Climbing should be a balanced set of movements, using solid
resting positions for the feet to take the weight off one's arms and
trying to move one hand or foot forward at a time, thus leaving
three points of contact with the rock.

It's not always possible to find suitable little projections for
holds. Sometimes the only way might be up a 'jam crack'—a smooth
crack without any projections where one tries to jam hands, feet,
body or sometimes even head, depending on the width of the crack.
One can use jammed fists and boots, or even have the whole lower
body inside and get up by a series of wriggles.

There can also be smooth, even vertical sections with neither
cracks nor projections. The technique for tackling this problem is
called 'friction climbing', relying on the adhesion of the climber's
rubber boot soles to the rock.

The leader has other things to think about too. A hundred and
fifty feet is a lot of rope, and a long way to fall. So the leader as he

progresses looks out for solid-looking belays to which he can attach the rope, which he does by putting one of his slings over the projection and clipping the rope to it with a carabiner. Now if he does fall he only goes down onto the sling.

Sometimes it may not be possible to find 'natural' or rock belays. In case of this, a leader might carry a bunch of pitons with him. These are metal spikes of varying sizes which are hammered into cracks. They have an eye in the head through which the carabiner can be passed.

He may do this a couple of times before he comes to a stance. A stance is usually—or ideally—a platform or some reasonably comfortable place where the leader can anchor and bring up the second man. The latter in his turn climbs the rock, *not* the rope, just as the leader did. He has about an inch or two of loose rope or 'slack' in front of him. If he gets into trouble, the leader pulls it tight. If he falls off, he just dangles on the rope, the leader holding him, as he is tied into the rock.

There is actually a method whereby the rope can be climbed, but most definitely not hand over hand. If a climber falls over an overhang and is held on the rope, unless he can climb back up it he's in trouble. The person who has held the fall can't give much help: he certainly can't pull the unfortunate up. Also, the hanging man has to act fast because it doesn't take too long to suffocate dangling on the end of a rope. To get out of this rough situation he uses a technique called 'prussiking'. Using a sling thinner than the main rope he can use a special wrap-around knot to attach himself to the rope. This is called a prussik knot, after its German inventor. The sling can be pushed freely up the rope, but when a downward pull is applied it sticks. By attaching two of these to the rope, and to himself, the victim can progressively slide his way up to the stance.

It's not hard to see why leading is that much more exciting than seconding.

In this way the climbers would continue to the top of the cliff. If they were of roughly equal skill then they would either swop leads or 'lead through', leap-frogging past each other. If one is better than the other, it's usual for him to do all the leading. When the pair have run out one length of the rope between two stances a 'pitch' has been established.

On reaching the top, a climb or 'route' would have been set up.

Now, obviously there are good climbers and bad climbers, and each person knows or should know roughly what his abilities are. To help people in this respect there are universal grades of difficulty or 'standards'. Every piece of rock is different. Some have large holds, some tiny, some are steep, some easy-angled; some vertical, some overhanging; some with cracks, some without. The experienced climber can read a piece of rock like a book, and when he climbs something for the first time he will give it a grading. This is something like giving a hole a par in golf: some will find it easier, some harder, but the standard is there as an average guideline.

Numerically, on the European system, grades go from 1 up to 6+ with high and low subdivisions of each standard. A rough table:

1: easy—E.   4: very difficult—V.D.
2: moderate—M.   5: severe—S.
3: difficult—D.   6: very severe—V.S.
                6+: extremely severe—E.S.

These are 'free climbing' gradings. So what is free climbing anyway? When a piece of rock is climbed without the use of pitons—this means without actually pulling on them, they can be used for protection—this is free climbing, as opposed to 'aid' or 'artificial' climbing, when pitons are placed and used for direct aid—pulled on, stood on or used to support slings which can then be stood in.

Artificial climbing—graded A1 to A5—is used to overcome sections that are not possible by traditional techniques, often roofs or overhangs. When cracks run out completely, bolts can be used. The climber drills a hole in the rock, hammers in an expansion bolt (something like the domestic Rawlplug), attaches a carabiner and proceeds in normal fashion. There are many rules, and many interplays between free and artificial climbing. A route that has been climbed free should never be done artificially, though vice versa is O.K. Bolts should not be used if a piton placement can be found, as extensive use of bolts could obviously destroy climbing. This is just touching on the ethics of the sport. Perhaps an easy summation is that you can always try to do better but never do worse. If you can't do what someone else has done without using unfair tactics, then it is more honourable to retreat.

'What goes up must come down.'

A simple, quite reasonable and oft-repeated question: how do you get back down once you have got up? Climbers are often likened to cats but this form of animal, though brilliant at ascending, is notorious for getting stuck and not being able to descend. Fortunately we do have methods which enable us to get down almost anything, given the right equipment.

The whole of the reason for climbing is the going up. Getting down is of course necessary, but instead of seeking difficult ways, invariably we look for the easiest. On most cliffs in Britain one can usually find an easy walk off the back. But say you have a tower, sheer on all sides—like the Old Man of Hoy, for example. You have reached the top—the easiest way up is Very Severe, there can be no walking off. How do you get down? To reverse climb a Very Severe pitch would be very hard and take a long time; the party does not consider it. The leader takes a piton, knocks it in until he's certain it will bear body weight, then ties a short sling through the eye. After this he takes the climbing-rope, threads it through the sling and coils the two ends together until he reaches the middle of the rope. He then throws or lowers the coils down the cliff until the weight of the rope is on the sling. First testing the piton with a pull, he wraps the rope round his body—or passes it through carabiners and then round his body—and slides down to the end of the rope. There are quite a few methods of wrapping the rope; the main idea is to get enough friction on the body, carabiner or descendeur—a special descending device—so that you can go down even overhanging rock in complete control.

The second man follows. Then they take one end of the rope and pull the other through, leaving the piton and sling at the top. And so on down the mountain. This is usually called 'abseiling', which is German for 'roping down'. It is a necessary but unpopular technique and provides one of the least good and most accident-prone sides of climbing. On the ascent, the climber is very much in control, he knows his abilities, places his protection and so forth; but in abseiling he has very little control over the situation. Everything is based on the piton or piece of rock which is the anchor point for the abseil. If this should come away—that's it. A high percentage of good climbers have been killed in abseiling accidents. A piton can work loose and what was secure for one man is sometimes not secure for another. Slings have been known to break or melt because of friction with the main rope, and there are many other tricks like going off the end of the rope or being left suspended half-way down an overhang without being able to get back in to the rock.

In these examples, I've been talking about small cliffs. But a mountain is just a series of cliffs, and the techniques used on the small are in multiplication what's used on the large.

Mountains, however, are not made only of rock. There seems to be a high proportion of snow and ice around, and the climbing of these substances is also an essential part of the sport. Here the climber becomes more like the heroes of fiction. Kitted up, he looks like something out of a medieval torture chamber. Muffled and gloved, he is usually seen wearing wicked spikes on his feet and carrying sharp instruments in his hands. However, the only torture inflicted is on the muscles of the users of these instruments. The spikes are called 'crampons'. A crampon is metal rim with either ten or twelve spikes between an inch and an inch and a half long, strapped round the sole of the boot. Twelve-point crampons are the best and most used, and in this case ten points go vertically downwards and the front two stick out like claws.

The hand weapons are ice-axes or hammers. These have shafts of varying lengths according to choice, but usually around eighteen to twenty-four inches, and a metal head with a pick on one side and either a hammerhead or an adze on the other.

With this equipment the climber has several ways of proceeding on ice. If possible he swings the axe or hammer so that the point sticks into the ice, and kicks with the front points of his crampons so they also stick in. By pulling up on the axe and balancing on his front points he can make his way up an ice slope. Sometimes, when the various points aren't sticking well, the climber chips out steps in the ice so that he can rest and progress more easily. The trouble with balancing upon front points is that it's strenuous and tiring; the compensation is that it's much quicker. Cutting steps, though safer, can be very slow and speed often counts.

There are pitons for ice as well as for rock, coming in two main types: straight drive-in and screw. The drive-ins are straight or angular pitons eight to ten inches long, and their holding-power is best when they actually freeze into the ice. When this happens, however, extraction can be difficult, and the person taking them out often has to cut away the ice right down to the point before he can free them. These pitons are useless in mushy ice.

The safest ice-piton is the screw type. There are three varieties of this. The original screw was something like a six- to eight-inch corkscrew with an eye for carabiner attachment in the end. These hold well in ordinary ice, but if it is at all brittle the screwing will shatter the ice around the piton and there will be no purchase. To counteract this problem the German firm of Salewa produced a different type of screw. This was tubular and hollow, with the threads on the outside of the lower part of the tube. On insertion the dis-placed ice would come up through the tube and the outside threads would grip the ice. There was no shattering and outward displace-ment as with the corkscrew type. The only problem with the Salewa piton was that in very cold conditions ice could freeze in the tube and make it useless. So a further extension was developed: the drive screw. This was tapering and solid with the threads on the outside and could be driven in and screwed out. This is the best all-round piton.

Ideally, the ice climber should carry a combination of these types in case he runs up against different types of ice. Conditions vary a lot more than they do on rock. There is straightforward snow, which one can virtually walk up, cutting steps to suit. An easy-angled slope is anything on an inclination from 0° to 40°. Between 40° and 60° is as steep as most people would like to handle and anything over that is for the very experienced only. But a 50° slope covered with snow or swaw ice can be that much easier than one covered with clear water ice. In swaw it's easy to progress and make steps. There's not so much strain on the legs. But moving up water ice is a demanding thing. Sometimes the points barely grip, and to cut even a small step can be a great effort.

Probably the worst ice that one can meet is black water ice. This is old stuff which has thawed and frozen time and time again until it reaches an almost rubbery consistency. Sometimes axes and crampons, unless especially sharp, simply bounce off this kind of stuff, and it can take a lot of work to make progress.

Verglas can also be very difficult. This is a thin veneer that forms on rock, caused by the thawing and re-freezing of running water or drips.

Finally, it should be noted that ice overhangs can be tackled on ice-pitons in the same way as rock overhangs on rock-pitons.

Take these techniques, take all the pieces of rock, snow and ice in the world, add a set of rules, and there you have climbing.

No—there's one more aspect I seem to have forgotten.
'Aren't you afraid of heights?'
'I get dizzy just walking up the stairs?'
Fear of heights, commonly but inaccurately known as vertigo, is something that is on every layman's mind when he talks to a climber. Nowadays I rarely notice the space around me—'exposure', as it is known—as I climb. Or, if I do, it's to savour it, enjoying the freedom. But I can do this only because I've grown accustomed to it. Initially it's a very strange thing to be poised above a drop, an alien thing, and I think most climbers are a little bit afraid at first. You know if you fall a hundred feet it could be very serious. But what about all these safety precautions, what about your ability? As confidence in these grows, fear of heights gets less. It seems to be something in our collective unconscious that heights make you dizzy and you fall. But why should standing on the edge of a cliff really be any more dangerous or make your head spin more than standing on the edge of a deep pool?

One has to conquer many inhibitions in climbing. In fact a little fear is a healthy thing—it keeps a sense of perspective. If it develops into panic, that's something else; but that involves loss of control, which is something that should never happen to a climber.

The only case of *genuine* vertigo I've seen in the mountains involved Don Whillans, my partner on Annapurna and Everest! This is a straight physiological thing due to a disturbance of the balance canals. He gets so dizzy he can't stand up. Psychological 'vertigo' can be overcome by patience, guidance and experience. Obviously there are many degrees of fear of heights, but for the one who suffers a lot, it is not an incurable thing, and when conquered provides vast new fields of potential enjoyment.

FRIENDS IN HIGH PLACES

A Sunday morning in May, aged seventeen. Stenhouse, Eley and I meandering around the loose rock problems of Caerketton in the Pentlands, just outside Edinburgh. A figure in red materializes.
'Hey! D'ye want tae dae some routes?'
'Why not?'
He looks competent. Medium height, dark haired, and moves like a fit man. Deep-set black eyes.

'Juist follae me an Ah'll show ye aroond.'

He climbs. We follow. Lots of climbs and we follow everything. Eventually, sitting on top of a crack:

'That's the fuckpig; the hardest thing here. We'd better go for a walk. I'm Jimmy Marshall.' Recoil by us. Marshall was one of the major Scottish figures. We'd heard many legends at Junior Mountaineering Club of Scotland (J.M.C.S.) meets, and we'd already met his younger brother Ronnie. Marshall and Robin Smith, the men who were into the fairy-tale world of the Very Severe. A friendship with Marshall developed that has lasted to this day. Sometimes I wonder why. Jimmy was twenty-eight, and already a qualified architect; we were seventeen-year-old roughnecks. Basically I think it was because he was at heart a roughneck himself. He had been weltering for years in the morasse of Scottish climbing politics. Except for the Creagh Dhu, a Glasgow working-class club whose membership was drawn largely from the shipyards, and who were considered beyond the pale, Scottish climbing was a mess of mediocrity and pettiness. It was full of mountaineers who considered their average talents to be exceptional. The main things in their lives seemed to be club rules, correct committee meetings and good etiquette in huts. These things are fine but climbing should have a place somewhere.

We, on the other hand, arrogant and uncouth but with unimpeachable climbing ideals, wanted to climb as hard and as well as we could to advance the state of Scottish climbing to where we could raise our heads with the rest of Britain and Europe. At that time, 1957, we were twenty years behind; we were rabid individualists. Marshall realized this, and in ourselves and Robin Smith I think he saw the chance of better days to come—in the next few years he himself was to climb much tougher things than he had before.

Perhaps the greatest influence in my early climbing career was Robin Smith. He'd already been climbing two years when we first met him. Hard routes in difficult conditions. Solo ascents. South Ridge of the Aiguille Noire at Chamonix, a difficult route for a British party at that time. You had only to whisper his name amongst the hangers-on whom we seemed to be hanging to and you would get in some climbing.

Again 1957, in August. Stenhouse and I lying in our tent on Gunpowder Green in Glencoe beneath the Buachaille. It was a

normal Glencoe day: the rain was skidding along horizontally, and
we were idly watching the rising river wondering if we'd have to
move our tents. Frustration was the mood. We'd spent precious
money taking a J.M.C.S. bus instead of hitchhiking as usual. It
looked like a wasted weekend. A head appeared in the door to
interrupt our mutterings.

'I'm Robin Smith. Would you like to go climbing?'

'Sure.' We never stopped to think why he would want to climb
with us. We got out of the tent to find a thick-set, medium-height
figure with incredibly bowed legs. He was dressed in the then
fashionable oilskin jacket, sou'wester and wellington boots.

'Where do you want to go?' say we.

He looks distant for a minute. 'There's a wee route on Slime Wall
called Revelation which could be interesting in the wet.'

We blinked. Having read the guide-book many times we knew
that Slime Wall was one of the steepest on the mountain, and that
Revelation was a V.S. on it. We had never done a V.S. . . . .
Ambition prevailed over caution.

'We only have welly boots and gym-shoes.'

'Ach, no problem. If you've got an old pair of socks you can stick
them over the gym-shoes. Leave the wellies at the foot of North
Buttress.'

Slime Wall on Buachaille Etive Mor starts half-way up Great
Gully. By the time we got to the start water was pouring out of our
ears and our welly boots like miniature ponds. The first pitch is a
traverse from a safe ledge straight out across the wall. First taste of
real exposure. Enjoyment was there despite our skidding feet. The
memories are still clear today of Robin taking hours over the second
pitch, yet I was not feeling unhappy as we stood belaying on a small
foothold each. Once or twice he slipped. Conditions—and his
decaying boots—were terrible; his climbing was great. We were
amazed at the quality of his equipment. It was as bad as ours. Four
old beaten-up slings with ex-W.D. carabiners and an old nicked and
scarred nylon rope. Some time late in the afternoon we were up.
Celebratory whoops and pushing boulders down into the depths of
Great Gully. Mud slides back to Gunpowder Green. Delighted with
ourselves, we were amazed in our naivety to see the jealous mind
in action for the first time.

'Madmen.'

'Could have been killed.'

'What would you have done if we had had to come and rescue you?'

No congratulations.

We found it strange that Robin Smith had such bad equipment. But on getting to know him better—and when my powers of character analysis had perhaps had some of the rough edges taken off—I realized that this was the way he played the game. This was his challenge. He had to increase the challenge by climbing at night, in the wet or sometimes solo, often in bad conditions and always with the worst of equipment. He hated artificial climbing.

His skill was immense. There was very little that really puzzled him on rock and ice. In early days he was unsure of these talents and often took a long time on certain climbs. This was not because of the technical problems: if someone told him that a climb by someone of repute was hard, he believed it, and consequently tried to find it so when it actually wasn't. It was a kind of mental insecurity block. When he got over this, which took about three or four years, he had developed into one of the best all-round climbers ever to come out of Britain.

I climbed with him steadily over a period of three years, but while we made a strong team and spent a lot of time socially together we were never really close friends. Robin had been to a public school, and often found it hard to shake the traditions of his good upbringing. He vandalized with the vandals, also part of the game, but I don't think his heart was really in it. He tried to steer a path on both sides—something I was accused of many years later, but certainly couldn't be at the time. His intelligence as an Honours Philosophy student was at the time away beyond that of his constant companions, Eley the engineer, Stenhouse the apprentice draughtsman, and myself the schoolboy and eventual student; but in practical experience of life he was a long way behind us, who were three years his junior. In a discussion on Kant or Hume he left us with blank faces; at a party we would leave him in the corner while we went after the girls. The advantages of a co-ed education.

In our climbing together it was always a game of each outstaging the other. Trying to steal leads, gain the hardest pitch, steal each other's gear. On one of the best climbs we did together, the first ascent of the Bat on Ben Nevis, we were barely speaking to each

other, having fallen out on an Alpine holiday when I didn't turn
up in Grindelwald to try the Eiger. In fact I'd had my money stolen
while hitching over and had to get home as quickly as possible. He
barely seemed to believe this. We only climbed together because
there was no one else around. If he had survived his trip to the
Pamirs, I think he would have made an unforgettable impression on
world mountaineering. He was only twenty-four when he died.

FIRST ASCENTS

Climbing in my early years was in the process of undergoing a very
important development. The available climbers had not yet
realized their talents to the full. There was a horde of eager up-and-
comings, and everywhere new rock and ice to climb. Scotland was
unknown in the climbing world at the time, but within a few years
it was to produce world-class climbers. Somewhere lurking in the
rain-soaked glens were the means and training necessary to reach
that level.

    Glencoe, the long dark valley of historical gloom. Entrance on
sweeping rainclouds and dark heather, horizontal sleet or high wind,
or—too rarely for the dedicated—a hazy purply day with the eye
sweeping from Buachaille Etive Mor down through the Three
Sisters of Gearr Aonach, Ben Fhada, Aonach Dubh to the gully-
scarred and scattered-buttressed Bidean. This was our hunting-
ground, easily accessible from Edinburgh by thumb, bike or, rarely,
car. We wandered, and found new dimensions. Incredible early
days, with standards to be heightened and so much unexplored
ground to look into.

    Winter would send us through the Glen and round the extra
forty miles to Ben Nevis. Many played on the slopes of Glencoe,
but the Ben had a more serious air. Trudging up the long walk and
into the jaws of the Corrie in winter or summer made one feel small.
Summer showed a glistening, often wet Carn Dearg Buttress,
probably the most impressive crag in Scotland. Long dark corners
with vivid green slime shining unnaturally bright in the rare sunshine. Winter brought a white mountain, with gully upon gully,
black ice, water ice, little avalanches blown by the wind; and usually
hiding like a coy lady behind a veil of cloud. But if the Ben was a
lady she was a true courtesan. Only practised lovers were allowed

to explore her fully. Competent and enthusiastic young searchers were drawn in and taught invaluable lessons. The ignorant and fumbling were totally rejected. We went and paid our homage with old favourite lovers and were slowly accepted and became lovers ourselves. Lessons taught, especially in winter on Ben Nevis, remain the true basis of the developed skills of today.

These were the early favourites. True, there were profitable visits to the other areas like Creag Meagaidh near Loch Laggan, the Cairngorms and the North-West Highlands, but our training-grounds were essentially Glencoe and Nevis.

It was an incredible situation for a young climber to find himself in. Our group had read all the exciting Alpine history. We wanted to be able to sample the experience of the great climbers, but the skills had to be developed right here in Scotland. This is no criticism of the many who love climbing on odd days and easy things, or wandering around the mountains. They are also true mountain-lovers. We were just a little more committed. By pushing our stand-ards we pushed ourselves and learnt more about both. This demands a hard, often ruthless state of mind. Often we didn't succeed on projects, but head-shaking we'd come back for more. The despised people were the ones who criticized through envy and because they were afraid to try the same things. There are always people who want a balanced mediocrity.

There were maybe about ten to fifteen people really active at this time. Split up into little geographical groups. Not only between groups but between individuals in each splinter section we were all in friendly competition. As a whole we stayed apart. Anti-social it has been called, but when one is disturbing comfortable fixed habits it is very hard to be popular. This attitude also keeps the positive drive intact, without any insidious infiltration of easy ideas.

Years later, in the mellowness of many mountain experiences, some of our behaviour at the time seems strange. But when you are unaware of your abilities, have grandiose plans, don't know if you can fulfil them, are moving in new social directions, fighting constant criticism and going through at the same time all the normal formative teenage problems then it is no surprise that what exists is a strange form of human animal. In all, a wild, crazy, sometimes disastrous period that was still a very essential part of shaping the mountaineer that I am now.

CHAPTER TWO

Scotland

Eley has a tremendous idea. Someone has offered him a prehistoric motorbike. Find twenty pounds—that's the only problem. Theoretically we shared it, but even a half-share was impossible on schoolboy pocket money. Eley was at least working and making money. He bought the bike.

It was no racing maching—a 350-c.c. Royal Enfield without even the benefit of telescopic front forks. All of two happy months we roared around. Then one fine May evening I was riding through Juniper Green in a great rush, flat out to make a date in town. I was doing complete maximum, which was around sixty-five, when there was a terrible shaking from the front forks. The next few seconds passed slowly. It got worse and worse until I couldn't control the handlebars any longer. The front wheel came right round; the bike stopped dead; I took off for new dimensions. My trip didn't last long. Sixty feet of propulsion. I had time to think when I was airborne. *No crash hat. Protect your head, Haston!* I curled my left arm around the valuable part and stuck out the right to take the force of the fall. The impact was rough. Skidding along leaving much skin stuck to the tarmac. Stop.

Amazingly, still conscious. Head O.K. but what's with my right arm? Hanging at a strange angle it was obviously dislocated. It had taken the full impact. By a stroke of fortune, or misfortune, I had landed right outside the local doctor's office. I limped in. He sent me to hospital. A few hours later I was back home with a fracture dislocation and multiple abrasions. That was the early summer finished for climbing.

Three worrying months followed. Just prior to the accident I'd been reading *Commando Climber*, an autobiography by the Marine climber Mike Banks. He had dislocated his shoulder and for years

19

afterwards had been plagued by the bone popping out when he was climbing. Eventually he'd had to have the thing pinned in an operation.

The thought of this worried me. I did not want this kind of thing to happen when my climbing was just developing. My physio-therapist was very sympathetic. I worked really hard on exercises, and the wasted arm became stronger. There was still trouble with lateral movement but pulling up seemed fine. The time of the big test arrived, and here I just about put myself straight back into hospital. Instead of breaking in gradually I followed Eley up Crows West Crack, a V.S. on East Face of North Buttress on Buachaille. Everything felt good, so I suggested that I lead Hangman's Crack, another V.S., just above. On this day it was to seem appropriately named. It's only one run-out of the rope. Two-thirds of the way there's a chockstone, a large boulder firmly jammed in the crack, for protection before the hardest part. I couldn't see the chockstone, so carried on anyway. The crux involves lay-backing and right hand pulling. Laybacking's hard work even with two good arms—it involves going up a corner crack with hands pulling against the edge of the crack and feet braced against the main wall. As it was, my arm was already too tired. Shaking and straining I fought it desper-ately. Down below the Creag Dhu were already taking bets and sharing out my boots and wristwatch. Somehow I pulled through but arrived pretty chastened on the ledge. I knew it had been very close. Not many people jump sixty feet at 65 m.p.h. and walk away. But I reckoned the only way to build up strength was to keep on climbing, and this I did, although with a little more caution. By September I was going really strongly again. The shoulder had healed well. I only experienced brief twinges in awkward jam cracks. I did what were then two of the hardest climbs in the Llanberis Pass, Cemetery Gates (in a lightning storm) and Hangover; then Gardyloo Buttress on Nevis, the third ascent with a new finish. All this proved that I was climbing as well as ever. Probably better, because I was doing a lot of leading and using techniques instead of relying on strong arms and a certain amount of gymnastic ability.

Our group spent every spare moment training. In Edinburgh it was the Currie Railway Walls and Salisbury Crags in the Queen's Park. It was forbidden to climb on the latter except for a few hours on Sunday morning, which we were never up to enjoy. But we

climbed anyway and added to the fun by having constant running
warfare with the park keepers. They could never run as fast as us
so we always got away.

Long walks in the Pentlands hardened the legs. By December it
was once again to Glencoe in search of winter snow and all the
different experiences involved in Scottish winter climbing.

It's Not All Climbing

Christmas '58. Eighteen-year-old Haston's bored. Wants to go
climbing but there's no one around. Not only bored but disgusted.
Robin's working at the Post Office. The rest of the mates have girl
friends and want to spend Christmas with them. Promises to go
away for the New Year but that's a piss up. Haston wants to go
climbing *now*. No money, probably a pound and no prospect of
more until after Christmas. Into mother's cupboard.

'She'll not miss this . . . . That looks good.'

'Cheerio.'

Out onto the well known hitching road. It's late and December
in Scotland. Darkness at four o'clock. After a few rides he's still
flagging forlornly at the side of Lock Lubnaig, a lonely spot half-way
to Glencoe. A truck pulls up. 'Glencoe, son? I'm going to Balla-
chulish.' Peace. Relaxation and sleepy diesel fumes. Too soon I'm
being woken up at the entrance to the 'Coe. It's a wild night but then
you seldom expect anything else in this part of the world. Drop off
at an unlit Cameron's Barn, an old cowshed at the foot of the
Buachaille.

'Ta, Jimmy.'

No lights. Oh well, better to be here alone than not at all. The
bedding is good. Straight concrete floor. Never even thought about
air beds or foam. There were so many other things to buy. Stick the
anorak down, out with the stove and straight into the bag. Soon
sipping tea and thinking of what I can climb alone tomorrow when
another truck pulls up outside. Voices. Glaswegian voices. two
figures burst in the door.

'Get the tea on, Jimmy.'

'Christ, it's you, Dougal.'

'What are ye daen here, china?'

'How's it gaun?'

My friends were John McLean and Davie Agnew of the Creag
Dhu. The Creag Dhu generally kept themselves to themselves and
gave Edinburgh people especially a hard time. But we had formed
close friendships with people like John Cunningham, Willy Smith,
Pat Walsh, McLean, Agnew and many others, based on reciprocal
drunken parties, all-night gambling sessions and tremendous climbing rivalry. Like us they hated pretension and loved climbing hard.
Hence the friendship—and the rivalry. Soon we were brewing up and
sharing tea and food. It was automatic that we should join up
together.

'Where'll we go tomorrow?'

'If it's fine we'll take a wander up the Buachaille. What about
Ravens?'

'Great by me.'

'If it's bad we can always go to the Fort. There's a dance there.
Might get a bird. The R.A.F. Rescue's there, we can always bum
rations from them, then go up the Ben.'

'How much money have you got?'

'About a quid.'

'We've got a thirty-bob kitty.'

'O.K. That's enough to buy some tucker and a few pints.'

'Christ, it's cold in here! I've only got a paper sleeping-bag. Let's
break into Lagangarbh.' Lagangarbh is the S.M.C. hut in Glencoe.

'Great idea. There might be some left-over food.'

No sooner said than the stoves and bags are packed and we're off
into the blizzard. Down a quarter-mile track. First man up goes
over the porch, fiddles with the skylight. It opens. We hand the
packs up and through into the warmth of the cottage. Beds, gas,
cookers, left-over food, we spend a luxury night.

In the morning the blizzard is still blowing. Christmas Eve. All day
to hitch to Fort William. It takes that. We meet again in the chip shop.

'Let's go to the pub and then the dancing.'

Considerable pints later we stumble into the dance hall. We're
scruffy and smell. Everyone's dressed up. No chance.

'Let's go to Glen Nevis and spend the night with the Rescue. We'll
get fed.'

Out into the blizzard again, a three-mile walk. Penniless this time.
Meet some mates, get fed up, sleep, and waken up to the same
weather. No point in trying to go up Nevis.

Back to Glencoe. We find a friend who's brought provisions for a week. Even a tinned chicken for Christmas dinner. The blizzard clears, but we have to go our separate roads home to get money for the New Year. That's how the game is played.

For me, it was back to the insurance office where I was working. I had an application in to go to university but the course did not start until June, so temporarily I had to earn some money.

Breaking The Ice

Life in insurance was appalling. I realized that I would be finishing in June, but that did not make the immediate present any more attractive. Often, sitting at my desk with work finished, nothing to do but having to keep up a pretence by doodling on proposal forms, I would find myself looking at the people around me. A room with maybe ten rows of clerks. The chief had started at the lowest end: forty years later he was at the top. I don't criticize. That had been his mountain. I tried to imagine myself climbing it. No way.

Back from thinking of other people's lives to the thoughts of my own future plans. This was the beginning of February 1959, and there was a two-week escape from insurance coming all too slowly: I'd asked for my annual holiday during that month. Everyone thought I was crazy.

'You'll be in the office all summer.'

'I'll think of you when I'm at the seaside.'

'Imagine spending your holidays ploughing around in the snow.'

At that time I hadn't told them I was leaving in June.

A Friday night, and off with the suit and into climbing gear, pick up the rucksack and leave the dire perils of loss of household effects behind. For this holiday it was a three-rope: Jimmy Marshall, Stenhouse and myself. Graham Tiso was coming for the weekend. What's more we had a car, a beaten-up old Ford with no heating. Even travelling in full climbing gear, it still needed a primus stove burning between the front passenger's feet to keep up any degree of heat. Skidding and ploughing his way through snowdrifts, Tiso made his usual erratic passage towards a barn at the foot of the Creagh Meagaidh.

The old man was plotting. He 'warmed up' with a harder route than anything on the mountain at the time, dragging a protesting

Tiso past myriads of escape ledges and always over icy bulges, to
make a route called Smith's Gully because Robin had had a previous
failure on it. He sent Stenhouse and me off to try and take some of
the kinks out of the Centre Post line, but we only followed ancient
footsteps and sneaked around the big centre bulge. Still, the
crampon muscles were moving. We didn't know how Jimmy
Marshall's mind was working at the time, but he was only using
this mountain for training. His eyes were on a winking Ben Nevis
gully, called by the highly unimaginative name of Minus Two:
the name might be rather common-place, but he knew the climbing wouldn't be.

A further fine day on the Creagh Meagaidh gave more training,
1,500 feet of meandering on Pinnacle Buttress through acres of
steep ice, snow, rock and frozen grass. Always through little bulges,
with the frozen loch a thousand feet below. It was my second day on
crampons. They were only ten-pointers, so there was no flashing
up on the fronts. At that time we knew only the Scottish style of
ice-climbing; a short axe, strong arms and lots of steps. Marshall
seemed to be able to cut steps like a simple and economical machine.
We weren't so adept, took much longer and weren't so good at
resting on steep ice.

When starting ice climbing I became aware of basic differences
in the learning of techniques. With rock climbing it had all seemed
reasonably natural, and I'd become good fairly quickly; with ice
there seemed to be so much more application and so many more
cunning little tricks to learn. But cramponning out that day at the
top of Pinnacle Buttress I felt it was beginning to come through a
little, and began to look forward to Minus Two.

The next night and a day's hitchhiking later Stenhouse, Marshall
and I were plodding up the frozen swamps of the approach to the
C.I.C. hut on Ben Nevis. This hut must be my favourite in Scotland.
It is very isolated: six miles from the Fort William road through bog,
river, snow, rain, lightning, sleet or even sunshine. We usually did it
at night so that a day's climbing wouldn't be missed. On a clear,
starlit winter night it was an incredible walk for contemplation.
Just the crack of the ice on the heather, the occasional shooting-star
and the stark beckoning whiteness of the Nevis Cliffs.

Many strange happenings took place on this path. People had
been known to lose the way and have to bivouac. Robin had split

his head in a three-hundred-foot slide when he'd mistaken a frozen waterfall for the path. Ronnie Marshall had threatened to swim up the river in January after leaving the Fort William pubs too late. It was always a walk of memories. We arrive to a crowded hut, but Marshall takes over in his usual fashion.

'They're all English. Scottish Mountaineering Club have first claim on bed space.'

So we move in. Mild splutters. Marshall is recognized, and he recognizes the English. It's the R.A.F. Rescue with their boss Ian Clough. In later years I was to become very friendly with Ian and do some good climbing with him, but at that time his deeds were generally disliked by our circle: 'An Englishman who put up lots of new routes and plastered them with pitons!' We also didn't have very much time for the routes he was doing in winter on Nevis. Later, we found out that they were usually fine and not difficult lines, but at that time we were very intolerant and also suspicious of any Englishman who thought he could climb ice.

This all seems unimportant and trivial nowadays, in the much more relaxed atmosphere we climb in, but at that time it was genuinely believed that only Scotsmen could climb ice.

The weather was great. Jimmy thought conditions were right, so Minus Two it was to be. Something we never seemed to get together in Scotland was early starts. Most parties would be up and off by first light. Usually our appointed cook would stagger up round eight and hand round the ritual tea in bed, and then everyone would embark on a series of messy rolls with sausage, bacon, egg, black pudding, so that you waddled out sometime in the mid-morning, well filled against the cold but often feeling distinctly ill due to the pound of greasy fat swimming around in your stomach.

That morning was no different. Three figures wandering solo, belching and cramponning to the foot of Minus Two.

The cirque of the Minus Buttress, Orion Face and Observatory Buttress is an impressive amphitheatre of rock, a great place for winter climbing. Long snaking fangs of beautiful snow ice sprouting everywhere, lots of them unbroken. Like going from bottom to top. Scenes of future experiences. At this time only Zero Gully had been climbed, a breakthrough in ice climbing by Tom Patey, Hamish McInnes and Nicol in 1957, but still waiting for a second ascent. The routes of Minus Two started uniform then diverged into

different paths half-way up. Jimmy's description tells the story
of our ascent:

'A winter ascent par excellence, the gully being barred by an
impressive ice bulge which proved a bit of an impostor. Difficulties
thereafter almost continuous. The left fork was followed to finish on
the crest of N.E. buttress, gained at nightfall. By the feeble light
of a crescent moon, stars and aurora the buttress was climbed. It
took eight hours; three pitons used for protection.'

For Stenhouse and me it was both a stunner and a mind-awakener.
We were supposed to share leads, but after we had followed Jimmy
over the bulge it became apparent that his experience and ability
were still beyond ours. We were taking as long to second as he was
to lead. I was still enjoying the climb, but realized that it was of a
standard beyond anything we had done at the time. After the
ardours of the gully, the finish up the North Buttress was an incredible experience. Wandering over classic and famous pitches in the
dark; whooping and shouting round the plateau to reach the hut at
2 a.m. The rest of the holiday consisted of more new routes, but
nothing to compare with that experience. In 1971, Minus Two
was still awaiting its second ascent.

Zero Gully

I woke up; the surroundings were spinning. It took me about five
minutes to realize where I was. My bed was a rolled-up curtain in
the S.M.C. clubrooms.

The previous night had been a wild party. I had no recollection of
going to bed but one thing was certain, there was a great hangover
lurking about. Dragging wearily and nauseously through a cup of
coffee, slow hazy memories began to infiltrate the alcoholic block.
Wightman had been there . . . . It was university vacation . . . .
Somewhere we were supposed to be meeting . . . Then it clicked. I
was supposed to be on route to the C.I.C. hut.

Climbing seemed so remote. It was three weeks since I had
touched rock. Easter exams and two weeks of stuffy libraries filled
with fear-soaked sweat of imminent failures and worrying certain
successes. Often I dreamt of climbing during the study hours as I
went through the almost futile motions of trying to get some other
kind of knowledge into my head. After the exams, the next week

degenerated into a round of celebrations and parties. Fabulous times with many strange happenings, but having to come to an end if you are basically interested in your health.

I looked around the usual haunts, but everyone seemed to be in hiding, nursing hangovers or girl students. Wightman seemed to have quit the city, so I decided to take a chance that my hazy memories were correct and head for Ben Nevis. Hitching was successful and my head started clearing on the walk in. Wightman was there brooding and sulking in the middle of a crowd of Oxford University types.

'You're late.'

'So what. You're lucky I'm here at all.'

Andy's not the most sociable person you could meet, so you have to treat him at his own level. We go into a huddle round the stove to get away from the English accents. Wightman grunts.

'What do you fancy doing tomorrow?'

'I don't know. I'm unfit. Need a good night's sleep first so fancy a late start.'

'I'm fed up with the classics. Let's go in head first. What about Zero?'

'Aw, Christ, O.K. If we start late we can always do the first pitch then finish it the day after.'

These few words seemed to go down well with Wightman as he resumed his sulky silence. I went to bed. I didn't seem to get much sleep, as the tramp of Oxford feet started about 5 a.m. and cleared away about 7.

Turn over. Wightman isn't that bright either as he gives me a cup of tea at 11 a.m. My head felt good but arms and calves were slightly feeble as we sauntered towards Zero. Memories of Minus Two as I looked across. No great bulges today, in fact hardly in winter condition at all. Only two years gone and it was no longer a virgin cirque, since Jimmy Marshall and Robin Smith had blitzed the Orion Face and Minus Three Gully. Zero looked blue and icy. Our equipment was still primitive—two short axes, some rock pitons but none for ice. The weather was fine but we were hopeless. A hundred feet was the limit of my work. There was a bulge above, and about twenty feet to go to the stance. But everything was weak. I thought of falling. That in itself is bad, it means your thoughts are wandering. There was only ice-peg protection possible, so none at all for us. Enthusiasm waned. It was a real low point. I didn't even seem to care. What had happened to the great urge? There was always tomorrow . . . . Arrogance diminished, we sat back at the hut listening to tales of great classics.

'Maybe we should have a warm-up route?'

Indecision was in the air when the door clattered open and a battered, dishevelled Robin Smith arrived. Another refugee from the party scene, it seemed. He sat giggling quietly as we muttered our failure. He'd spent the last two days in the bed of a long-sought-after friend and was full of satiated complacency.

Mutterings from us about him climbing solo on the morrow.

Pondering quietly he suddenly came out with:

'There's a new route to go on Gardyloo Buttress. But it seems a pity to waste the steps you've cut. Let's have a three up on Zero tomorrow.'

Suddenly it began to seem right after all. Pessimism fled and I quickly agreed. A quick look at our equipment revived doubts.

'Where's your rope, Smith?'

'Forgot it. It's in Edinburgh.'

It's slightly awkward to do full run-outs with three people on the rope. Shifty eyes round the hut. Plenty of ropes hung up. Whispers: 'Let's wait until they've left in the morning and borrow one. They're bound to have spares.'

'Any ice-pegs?'

'No, but Marshall and I used the hut poker before. It's all right.'

The poker goes into the rucksack.

Predictably, the early-morning masses leave at the same time. I nip up quickly. There's a couple of ropes. Into the rucksack then back to bed again.

This time no one wakes up. Panic around noon, with breakfast for lunch. It's 2 p.m. before we stand at the start. Five hours of daylight left. It was in much harder condition than when it had been done first. Then it had taken five hours in superb snow ice, but now it was water ice: 400 feet of difficulties then 900 feet of snow gully to the summit plateau. Robin reckoned if we were over the difficulties by dark then we could easily climb out—needless to say, a torch wasn't part of our tools. But there again climbing on Ben Nevis in the dark was not an unusual thing. Robin moved off. Yesterday's steps were still available, as there had been no wind to fill them in overnight. Robin reached the end of the old steps, banged in the hut poker for a rest, cut round the bulge and there was the stance. But even that had taken two hours.

I moved up as quickly as possible and let Robin lead on the next pitch; he still seemed to be moving better than I. Wightman was shivering, still at the bottom and not destined to move for another couple of hours. The angle was still high, another hundred feet to a little recession where the gully twisted to the right. I took over, warmed up by this time, and got to the beginning of the last pitch in the grey dusk. The others came up. We sat in a contemplative huddle looking at the bulges ahead.

There was still some light as Robin moved off again. This time everything seemed to click for him; he was cutting like a precision machine. The rope rocketed out. This was really high-quality ice climbing in action. We followed in the dark, fumbling to find holds as a wind was now blowing some spindrift around. Theoretically the difficulties should have ended there, but that would have been too simple. Because of the lateness of the season and the lack of ice the exit to the gully was by no means obvious. What should have been a straightforward snow slope was now icy mixed ground. It took us eight hours of highly interesting wandering before stumbling onto the summit plateau.

Night climbing is something that people should try more often. There is a great feeling of being alone. Difficulties are greatly distorted. Quite often a small chockstone takes on the appearance of a huge bulge. It's a constant groping movement, with none of the enjoyment of space and exposure you get during the day but a very strong feeling of being in very strange surroundings. Shattered violently on reaching the plateau by shouts into the night. Spontaneous releasing of nervous energy. Then down, to another day.

BAT

September 1959, and I'd been accepted for university. That meant a government grant in October. What to do in the meantime? My insurance office employment was useful at last: registered unemployed, two pounds ten shillings a week. More than enough to live in Glencoe. The only trouble was that the bureaucrats did not seem to have taken unemployed climbers into consideration when they made the rules, and I had to hitch down twice a week to sign on, otherwise no money. They also kept offering me jobs. Fortunately, because of the proximity of university, I was virtually unemployable.

Robin Smith and I were the only ones around. For once he'd passed his exams in June and didn't have any resits in September. We were in one of our non-talking moods but climbed together anyway. You don't actually have to spend much time together when climbing—usually there's a separation of rope and rock. There was an exciting prospect on Ben Nevis awaiting the right conditions. Carn Dearg Buttress holds three great corners. Two of them had been climbed—what was more, by English parties. This was still rankling, and Smith had already made an attempt on the central, unclimbed line. He hadn't been able to reach the corner and reduced his frustration by climbing Sassenach and Centurion, the other corners, in the one day. Now his partner had gone back to Edinburgh to resit exams, and our paths seemed destined to collide once again.

On the Sunday we made our usual noonday start on a training climb. Darkness and drizzle saw us out of the end of Carnivore, one of the hardest climbs in the Glen and doubly pleasing for me after an ignominious failure earlier in the year when I hadn't been able even to get off the ground. My climbing at that time seemed to go in erratic patterns: the previous day I'd led a new route on the nose of Great Aonach, yet on Carnivore I just couldn't move. But the ascent with Smith removed the black mark.

There was now only one object in both our minds: the lurking, hanging corner on Carn Dearg. So it was off on the road round to Fort William. Somewhere on the way we lost a lot of hours and reached Fort William too late to buy food. This reduced our time, as I had to be back in Edinburgh on the Wednesday to collect my dole. Crashing that night in a garden shed, we planned to leave early next morning carrying only slings and pitons and try to blitz the route in a day. Brazen optimism, thought I, as we found ourselves at one o'clock next day at Smith's high point, still separated from the main corner by an ugly, winking little overhanging groove. I could see Smith's mind whirling and scheming. He offered me the groove. This wasn't generosity: he was obviously planning to lead the big corner. At this time I was indifferent. The one looked as hard as the other and the groove would have to be done.

Not even answering, I grabbed all the gear and moved up the

groove. It really pulled out the works for me. To make an exit at the top I had to put a sling on a small spike, stand in it, then pull up onto poor holds above. I moved up, the sling rolled off. Only up now, or a fall down. I hauled out onto the ledge above with my arms completely knotted up. Smith came up, slowly for him, and I knew he'd found it hard as well. He didn't say much; just collected the gear and went straight into the corner. It was impressive all right. A damp crack running up to an overhang, with a long mossy crack disappearing out of sight above. A long pitch with none of it looking simple and lots of moss and grass to be cleaned up before holds could be found.

He had slowed right down. It didn't take too long to reach the roof but there he squatted for a long time like a metal-festooned crow, only sidling out periodically to look over the edge, taking a sharp glance then retreating back to his nest again. One prolonged sally produced a wooden wedge out on the lip. Oh-oh, I thought, knowing his dislike for means artificial. Testing it, he pulled up, then announced he was coming down and I could have a try. This really put me on guard. What was over the edge?

A quick changeover. The day was pushing on; I'd have to try to move more quickly. A half-hour of violent contrast followed. I reached his high point without any trouble and felt like rubbing the fact in, but fortunately refrained. About forty feet above the roof, there seemed to be a grassy ledge. I decided to go, always thinking I could stop and bang in a piton if things got bad. In my over-confidence I'd hopelessly underestimated the angle of the corner. Overhanging it was, and my ledge didn't exist. I found myself with fingers stuck despairingly into a turf that was sliding. I tried to put something in, but my hand was opening in the mud. Seconds later I was flying head first through the pure Ben Nevis air and over the bulge to a terrible jerk which turned me upside down and left me there, spinning. Looking down I saw a face inches away from mine: Smith, not looking so cool as usual. The wedge had held, but he'd been pulled off his stance and we were both hanging from it. Various swings and contortions got us back on to the rock. It was now almost dark. There was no way of making it that day, so it had to be retreat. Even that wasn't simple. Beneath us the rock overhung for much more than the length of our rope. The only thing to do was to traverse down and across Sassenach, to where we thought there was a retreat point around 150 feet high. Robin led, fumbling; and still shattered, I followed. Down went the rope. The only way to find out if it reached was to follow.

Total darkness. I set off. Half-way down my anorak rips. Swinging free, there's nothing I can do. Nylon to bare flesh for seventy feet. It's O.K. for length. I squelch up to my knees in mud at the bottom, wondering if my neck is still attached to my body. Robin spins down, and we slink off defeated into the night. He nursing his frustrated dreams. Me thinking only of burnt flesh.

How easily hardship is forgotten! The next weekend we were back in Glencoe plotting another attempt. A lucky visit to the Saturday-night pontoon school saw us slinking out the Glen with pockets full of notes, enough to try a week-long siege if necessary. But we went chasing girls and watching films, ended up once again in our back-garden shed, and then got to the hut so late on the Monday that we slept right through to mid-day Tuesday and were only awakened by a huge crowd of ramblers passing the hut.

Blinking in the mid-day sun, we rushed at the buttress, and seemed to forget about difficulty, because we were back at the foot of the corner within an hour and a half.

Smith's turn again. Four hours, two pitons and two falls later, he was above my ledge and the difficulties. The first leap had been the result of a pull on the not-so-faithful wooden wedge. Trustingly standing in a sling attached to it, he'd looked down to find it moving. A few seconds later and the positions of the week before were violently reversed: he was upside down looking at me. Next time round he was hanging on a piton when it also decided to remove them both from the corner. Back to square one. But Smith was incredibly persistent. A last try—everything held—he was up. I followed in the twilight, leaving everything in place to save time, and led through in a long dusky groove to bring us out without too much hardship at the top of the corner. Unfortunately the top of the corner was still some 500 feet short of the top of the buttress. Retreat was unthinkable. Bivouacs also. It gets cold on September nights on Ben Nevis. Especially in shorts and sweaters.

Robin reckoned he could climb the upper part of Sassenach in the dark. He led, I followed. The moon kept teasing us. It was out but to the left of the line of corners we were climbing. The corners always stayed in the shadows. We didn't worry too much. One of the best routes on Nevis was in the bag and we both enjoyed night climbing. Singing and calling to the moon, we wandered up the Sassenach grooves, and got back to the hut at five in the morning. To put an end to the saga, I came back the next weekend with Marshall while Smith was sitting in exams. Climbing to the top of the main Sassenach chimney, we moved left to the top of the Bat corner and finished up a glorious line of grooves to make a fantastic route which lacked only an all-in-one ascent.

We called it the Bat, for a few reasons, but mainly because of the swooping falls over the roof and the constant night climbing.

CROSSWAYS

Traversing—going across a cliff from one side to the other—often seems even more pointless to laymen than an ordinary climb. While I don't take the view that getting to the top is everything, I would agree that to go from one side to the other never gaining the top is too much.

I remember a cliff in Glencoe that attracted a few seekers of the crossways. In actual climbing, girdle traversing is usually reserved until most of the straight-up lines on the cliff have been done, and on the West Face of Aonach Dubh there was a huge cliff with some remaining lines to be climbed. But the starts of these were usually wet, greasy, overhanging and covered with moss. The cliff was around 400 feet high, and about mid-height the rock was drier and grease free. We reckoned that to cross the cliff would give a thousand feet of climbing, equivalent to two and a half straight-up routes and sufficient to turn us from the vertical to the horizontal. There were a lot of teams eager to do this climb. It was perhaps the greatest plum left in the Glen. The Creag Dhu in particular were livid that we'd plucked a series of the finest lines in Glencoe—they didn't like continuously having to do second ascents. Especially ones that they had trouble on, so they couldn't come down and tell us they were easy.

Even the atmosphere in Edinburgh was bad; everyone splitting into little groups and plotting. Somehow Robin Smith and I were speaking again, and one cold April day we were up and away into the slimy shadows of Aonach Dubh.

The start looked wild. From Ossian's Cave a crumbling, very

steep white wall blocked off the first part. As we were sitting medita-
ting this piece of nastiness, Glaswegian voices disturbed the thoughts.
We were hidden but our rucksacks were at the bottom. Quietly we
peered over the edge: it was John McLean and Davy Agnew. We
could see them muttering and looking around. A beeline was made
for the rucksacks. Robin stood up.

'Piss off, you're too late!'

Their faces were beautiful. Obviously up to try the girdle, they'd
thought the rucksacks belonged to tourists climbing into Ossian's
Cave. A terrible beating of the English language ensued. At last
McLean calmed down enough.

'We'll eat your chocolate anyway.'

We'd left some apples and chocolate in the rucksacks. Looking
round for something to throw, my eye picked on the Visitors' Book
wrapped in the metal case. My hands seemed by magic to take hold
of it and hurl it at the two below. Robin rolled rocks. They scattered,
swearing and threatening great revenge. They had our chocolate
but we still had the climb. (In case anyone wonders what happened
to the Visitors' Book, here is my written confession.)

We were all day on the White Wall. I led into the middle; Robin
led out. By night we were in a rattling loose crack called Fingal's
Chimney, which had been climbed a few years before. There was
no way out but up. Hours and hours we fumbled up, then across
Pleasant Terrace and back to our empty rucksacks around ten.
The usual Glencoe weather set in. Steady drizzle, a waist-high wade
through the river and a five-mile walk saw us back at the hut, too
exhausted to be able to think of going back on the fine day which
naturally followed.

Smith returned with Wightman and added two more vegetation
pitches. Others were sniffing around, but the climbing was hard and
the weather usually bad.

In 1961 I came back with Robin Smith for another attempt. We
were climbing really well. Early in the day we had done two more
pitches. Full stop. What confronted us was one of the nastiest pieces
of rock either of us had seen: an overhanging wall, completely
undercut and about a hundred feet long, separated us from the
next ledge system. It was too much. Disillusioned, we scurried off
down Pleasant Terrace and called the route impossible. We should
have known better. 'Impossible' is a dangerous word to use in

climbing. Everyone thought it was a ploy to keep rivals away from
the route. They knew we'd come up against something really hard,
but thought we were only resting till we could get it together for
another attempt. For once, though, the story was true.

I almost dismissed the route from my mind. Robin kept thinking
but did not make any more attempts. It took a year before the next
one, and this was the first in which neither Robin nor I had been
involved. The two Marshalls romped over to the 'Barrier' pitch
and also retreated, customary arrogance slightly diminished.

We were all at Lagangarbh. I'd just done the second ascent of
Smith's Big Top on Aonach Dubh. Jimmy didn't reckon he'd go
back to the girdle, and I still didn't have my old enthusiasm. The
door opened, Smith lurched in. He turned in quickly to the conversation, and a strange look came across his face.

'Do you fancy another try?'

'Me? No, I'm going to Marshalls Wall tomorrow.'

He knows better than to try persuasion. Turning unabashed to
Ronnie:

'What about you?'

Ronnie's always easy and doesn't really seem to care what he
does. It was just as well. He spent eight hours sitting on a slab the
next day as Smith cracked the Barrier. It was another finish in
darkness, so Ronnie couldn't follow and all the essential gear was
still in the pitch.

A repeat scene next night in the hut. Ronnie and Jimmy were off
to Edinburgh; they had to work. My second man was off too.
Resistance began to crack. Smith wanted his gear back—he
reckoned the climb was in the bag. There was another strong two-
some, Rob Campbell and Niel McNiven, in the hut, otherwise
only student layabouts left. A few beers in the Kingshouse was
enough to make it a foursome. Smith reckoned I should lead the
Barrier so we split into two twos: McNiven and I, Campbell and
Smith. I knew he'd found it hard when he was insisting I try it—
eight hours is a long time for a hundred feet. Perhaps he thought I'd
fall off.

Early next morning we were up and moving fast through the
slimy shadows to the foot of the wall, Neil and I ahead leaving the
other two arguing about who should wear the one pair of P.A.'s.
(These are special boots for hard rock-climbing, with stiff, smooth

rubber soles and canvas uppers. The initials are those of their inventor, Pierre Allain, a famous French climber before the Second World War.) Reckoning I'd done the first part at least three times, and wanting to be fresh for the Barrier, we scurried up Pleasant Terrace and down to the start of the fearsome pitch.

It was a classic piece of Smith. He hated using pitons, but this time the rock had squeezed three from him. In between were a series of slings on little spike moves. The last part was a brute of an overhanging crack that kept on going to a violent pull onto a ledge. As hard as anything I'd done in Glencoe, but I wasn't going to tell him. They caught up quickly, mumbling about ethics and incomplete ascents—they'd started at Ossian's Cave. I closed Robin up by asking why he'd taken so long on the Barrier, and once again we'd needled each other into a state of open warfare. Livid, he did it in about fifteen minutes, a great piece of climbing. I scuttled off into the unknown before I had to tell him so.

Campbell was the unlucky one who had to take the pins out. It was too much: I caught a glance of a pair of feet swinging violently into space then back in again. Prussik knots saw him up. The rest was Very Severe but great climbing, and we enjoyed ourselves so much that we even finished up in daylight and were all talking happily to each other.

CHAPTER THREE

The Dolomites

Innocents abroad. We were going to try at last to make our presence felt in the Alps. There had been very little planning: Marshall had just said quietly one day that we should go to the Dolomites with him that summer.

The Dolomites are an area of limestone mountains in Northern Italy. Lower than the Western Alps, they get much better weather. We'd read many descriptions of huge yellow walls rising above grassy meadows and pine trees. In climbing history they had played a very important part, and many of the techniques that led to the climbing of the great Western Alp faces were discovered and developed in this traditional testing-ground. The principal climbing areas are the Tre Cime de Laveredo, near Cortina; Marmolada, the highest Dolomitic mountain, near Misurina; and the Civetta range, above the village of Alleghe. Other less known but excellent climbing ranges are the Catinaccio near Bolzano and, in the south, the Brenta Dolomites.

All names. Minds full of stories of Cassin, Comici, Solleder, the local heroes; we just had to go and have a look for ourselves.

The party was initially Jimmy Marshall, brother Ronnie, Eley and myself; a last minute addition was John McLean. Arrangements were to hitch to London, spend a night in a jazz club, then catch a train to Bolzano. This, amazingly, we did successfully; and despite hassles with Dolomitic bus-drivers we got ourselves to a bivouac place at the foot of the Vajolet Towers in the Catinaccio region without having lost anything or anyone.

The airy Grade 4 towers were traversed, and our minds immediately shot into outer spaces. Jimmy Marshall was making the decisions. 'Tomorrow we go to the Marmolada, bivouac and try the South Pillar.' I blinked. Buhl had had a terrible time getting up this thing. Though done as early as 1929, it was still a genuine 6,

37

and the upper chimneys had a bad habit of being heavily iced, always epic when you are only prepared for rock climbing.

Pre-dawn, and stumbling through constant reminders of war: dug-outs, barbed wire, shell-cases. The Ombretta Pass, where the pillar starts, had been a sought-after point in the First World War. It cost many lives. I tried to think how the victorious party would have profitably used it. And my eyes and thoughts wandered towards the pillar, the object of our own useless aspirations. Still, at least we were only involving ourselves.

Ten hours and many pitches later Jimmy and I were in the exit couloir, the gully at the top of the pillar, completely sodden. The last pitches had been wet cracks, with wooden wedges to be gripped like soggy Mars bars. Ice flashed above as the sun began to move around the corner; the famous crux chockstone glistened overhead; an occasional icicle smashed past. It was here that Buhl had experienced a feeling of almost going beyond it all and where Don Whillans suffered a few extremely pensive moments some years later. Going on for once didn't really enter our heads—P.A.'s don't have fur-lined inners.

Down it was. Abseils into the lower rope. A few words of explanation and 1,500 feet of long, out-hanging, body-burning abseils. One rope stuck half-way down. This meant another try, or at least a retrieving move. Another day. Sunset saw the last soaked, miserable figure sitting amongst the debris of two different types of warfare. Long stumbling marching brought us to our camp amongst the trees, and a fine appreciation of the beauties of a pine needle bed. One of the many things that one normally takes for granted.

I couldn't eat, only drink. Eley and I drank so much water that we spent the whole night being sick. A good introduction to the harder climbs. Rest was for a day when Marshall suggested retrieving the rope: the semi-old recover quicker than the young, something I found out in later years but didn't appreciate then. Secretly, I think, he wanted to finish the climb but he was cool enough to see that I was still mentally and physically tired, so we freed it and went down and left the Marmolada. Arrogance very much on the wane.

Visiting the Tre Cime de Laveredo helped pull the confidence round. An unforgettable first impression. Round a corner and there they were.

'Jesus Christ!'

Everything looked three miles high. Yet, after a warm-up, Eley, Ronnie and I were soon muscling up the North Face of the Cima Grande by the Comici route. In 1959 it did not suffer from the crowds that it does now—at present you probably have to bivouac 300 feet up to be the first party. We were alone.

Our artificial climbing then was still very slow: the odd piton in the railway walls was not sufficient training for the Cima Grande. Still, it was a good place to learn. In the Dolomites, nearly all the pitons are usually in place so initially it's just a case of moving ladders and getting used to incredible exposure. Lots of tourists gathered below. No watches, so I shouted to ask the time. Late. Let's move. We'd finished the overhanging section. My hammer sling broke and scattered the watchers. We rushed up the final ring band to a bivouac on the top. Lost the way as usual in the morning, but got down eventually to find happy Jimmy and John, who had just done the Cassin route on the North Face of the Cima Ovest.

By this time we were slim and fit. *Very* slim—the basic diet was corned beef, spaghetti and tea. Each of us had brought six tins of corned beef with him from Britain. In the valley, we gorged on milk and cheese to prevent a breakdown in the physical motor. I had around twenty pounds, and planned to be away for two months. A hard life, but good training for future mountain starvation.

After the Marmolada and Tre Cime, there was one more must: the Civetta. We left for Alleghe, a beautiful little village which sells the best ice-cream in the world and lies directly beneath the Civetta's North Face.

Sleeping out in the local graveyard we planned the days ahead. Marshalls and McLean to the Solleder route on the Civetta; Eley and I to the North-West Face of the Valgrande. Both hard pre-war classics. The others got up in a storm, but we failed miserably on two consecutive days, first when we followed the wrong approach and ended up on the wrong mountain, then again when Eley felt ill at the start of the difficulties. Two retreats, then right down to Alleghe for ice-cream to restore our bruised egos.

Stumbling into the graveyard we couldn't find our rucksacks. Panic. No passports. Using our best Italian—three words—we were eventually directed to a police station a few miles along the road, where we explained our predicament in English. The fat chief sat at his desk scowling.

'What nationality?'—in Italian.

Working it out by signs I answered, 'Scottish.'

At this his face burst into a wide smile and he thumped a bell on his desk. Straight away a policeman with automatic rifle at the ready came bursting in the door. Christ, I thought, what's happening? Eley was looking very cagy—he's big and strong, but not that strong. He looked at the window, then at the gun. Our faces stayed expressionless. A few rapid orders and our friend heel-clicked out.

Silence. The chief twiddles his thumbs. We wait for the handcuffs. A knock on the door. In comes the other, with rifle slung over shoulder, clutching not handcuffs but two litres of red wine and four glasses.

'Cheers to Scotland.'

Those two litres and another one later we staggered out, clutching a Carte Blanche to the whole of Europe, signed and stamped about twelve times by the Commissioner of Alleghe. Haters of authority that we were, our minds couldn't quite grasp it all. Nineteen years to find a friendly policeman. We collapsed in the graveyard, to find the gravedigger had stored our sacks in the mortuary. He was friendly as well, and offered us a bed in the same place. Politely we muttered excuses about the Civetta and fled to our high camp on the hill.

That night there was a big lightning storm. We wondered about the whereabouts of the others. Later we found out they were bivouacked in the upper chimneys of the Solleder, thinking of the poet-climber who had been drowned there in the thirties. Morning was bright and sunny and we hesitated about what to climb. We couldn't take another Valgrande attempt. Leafing through the descriptions we found Cima Su Alto—'one of the hardest climbs in the Dolomites; Grade 6+'. Fed up with failure but still strangely confident in my ability I looked at Eley.

'We may as well try that. If we're going to fail again let's do it in style at least.'

He just shrugged his shoulders. 'Why not?'

The description mentioned one bivouac, maybe two. Our equipment was first class! Rope, carabiners, water-bottle, two apples, extra sweater for bivouacs and a great will to succeed. Reckoning on bivouacking at the foot of the climb we ransacked the camp. One tin of corned beef. 'At least we'll eat well tonight,

then we'll just have to climb quickly before the effect wears off.'
Thus rationalizes Eley.

For the bivouac we would at least have our sleeping-bags, but
they would be left at the bottom. Two hours later the bags were
full and lying down beneath a rock. Above in the twilight the clean-
cut diedre of the Su Alto. It starts a third of the way up the face.
All the main difficulties were there, with easy ground to start. A
beautiful starlit night. We lay marvelling under the stars, excited
but happy. I began to experience what was to become a normal
feeling before big climbs in later years. A difficult climb made it all
seem worth while. It would be total commitment. I looked forward
to the abatement of the excitement of the night, to the total calm
and concentration when you actually start onto the rock.

The twilight hours, and movement. What movement! Failures
forgotten, we seemed to climb incredibly smoothly. By 9 a.m. we
were in the diedre. Even that flowed past: roofs, bulges, cracks, no
problem. At 7 p.m. I led out a rope length and there was flat ground.
It had been an incredible day, the first time that I had been so
totally involved in concentration and movement. Sheer, simple,
basic happiness. What a way to find it—climbing an overhanging
ladder of rusty nails! Was this what the Utilitarians had been
looking for?

Darkness comes early in the Dolomites, so we just lay down on the
flat summit and waited for morning. Bivouac equipment: shirt,
sweater, anorak, jeans, P.A.s, no socks, no food, a little water,
happiness.

How often it seems we live in a world of violent contrasts! Around
midnight, a few drops of wet in the sky. More and more and more.
What could we do? There was nothing to do. Five hours to daylight, and we just lay there getting wetter. Dawn—grey, cloudy,
still raining heavily. Immediate descent.

I looked at the description. No mention of the descent route. We
had noticed this before, but reckoned if we could get up the thing
there would be no problem getting down. Was this the punishment
for our naivety? We were shivering violently, and the only survival
was movement, so we headed towards the south side. After about ten
minutes Eley found an old peg with some slings in it, sure signs of a
way down. We tied in a new sling, threw down our double rope,
and I started down. Twenty feet . . . then space. Straight over a

large overhang. I couldn't see the bottom and kept going, foot after foot, but still nothing. Then a solid substance, not the rock I was looking for but a solid wall of water pouring over the edge. A blur in the mist—at last! There was a chockstone. I got off the rappel but couldn't turn the water off. There was no hiding from it. If you got out of the waterfall the wind-driven cold rain made you shiver just as much. Abseil after abseil. Then, with two of us on a ledge:

'What's up, Eley?'

'Can't move the rope.'

We both grabbed an end and jumped. Still no movement. This really looked like trouble. There was no sign of the bottom, though the overhangs had relented. A last try: nothing. I went back up but could only manage forty feet before the overhang. So out with the hammer, a few blows, and we had two 40 foot ropes instead of two 150-foot ones. We decided to avoid abseiling again unless it was inevitable, and started climbing down. Neither of us said anything, but both knew well that if there was one more bad abseil . . . We chased the thought away. Suddenly a ledge, and a break in the cloud. In the distance I could see slabs. Euphoria.

Blinding down, I was suddenly halted. There was an overhang beneath. The cloud had come in again. We had to try it: in with a piton, double the rope and off I go.

Very quickly the ropes end. I look down. A vague blur beneath— thirty feet or sixty? Who knows? I jump. Violent shock. Then the adrenalin boils over. I'm O.K.

'Come on, Eley. It's only about a ten-foot jump.'

The clouds lift. A few slabs, then green grass. Eley jumps.

'To hell with the ropes, let's go.'

Green pastures, a long valley, a never-ending walk and we were out. A total climbing experience.

DIRETTISSIMA

I developed a liking for the Dolomites, especially for the Tre Cime area, the scene in the late fifties of some very important developments in climbing.

In the Dolomites, as in the rest of the Alps, the aim of the climber had always been to follow the natural lines on mountains. Throughout the years there had been a logical progression: first the easiest ways up a peak, then the harder ridges and faces, and finally the hardest faces.

The Dolomite and eastern Alpine climbers had always been foremost in developing new techniques. The feeling here by 1955 or so was that most of the great natural lines had been followed. What to do? Stop climbing? The eyes of the modern thinkers turned towards the unnatural or direct lines.

This was when the famous or notorious word *direttissima* began to appear for the first time. The idea was to climb as directly as possible towards the summit, or tackle blank faces and large overhangs. There are often many blank spaces between natural faults in these lines. To fill in these it was necessary at first to use large numbers of expansion bolts and to develop a higher technical standard of piton work. This kind of thinking caused a great ethical trauma in the climbing world, as new techniques invariably seem to. Most lead climbers only want to use bolts when they really have to. But if a magnificent new route came out of having to fill in a few blank gaps by bolts—why not? People began to be so aware of placing bolts that a new technical standard of artificial climbing arose; though this was not manifest in Europe at the time it was growing in America, in the Yosemite valley. I shall go more fully into this later.

The Tre Cime first felt the wind of climbing change in 1958–59. The Germans established a direttissima route on the Cima Grande. Then two new lines were made on the face of the Ovest, one by Swiss–Italian teams taking the left side of the huge overhang, the other by the French on the blank wall on the left of the roof, called the 'Couzy Route' in memory of a great French climber.

In 1959, on our first visit, we were amazed at the activity at the foot of the faces. Base camps, ground support teams, girl friends, radios. Climbers usually hauled their supplies up at night, by long trailing ropes which went down to their base camp. Hot meals and sleeping-bags at the end of a day's work: we couldn't believe the equipment as we walked past in our ragged boots and jeans.

With the accomplishment of these routes, it was considered that there was a new standard in the Dolomites. They were said to be a grade harder than things like Su Alto or Scottoni, though at the time

the hardest of all—the Phillip–Flamm on the Punta Civetta—was
still in hiding, awaiting its second ascent.

But they were hard all right. Repetitions were rare. In 1961 the
routes were still in their teens. This gives an indication of the
difficulty, as the Tre Cime is the playground of the Dolomites.
When something new and hard is done, there is usually a queue of
climbers waiting to repeat.

In 1961 Robin and I decided that we were ready for a crack at
one of these three routes. His Alpine qualifications were now impressive: West Face of the Blaitière, Walker Spur on the Grandes
Jorasses. I had added to my previous list the Cassin Route on the
Cima Ovest and a few Alpine classics, but still not a major Alpine
route. Confident as ever, we decided on the overhang of the Cima
Ovest by the Swiss–Italian route.

For once the organization had been good. The trip was planned
in the pubs of the pea-fields of Kent, where we had been supple-
menting our meagre incomes in order to be able to go on holiday
for the Alpine season. Robin was shovelling peas outside Maidstone
and I was in a warehouse in town. Long, boring days with much
overtime to boost wages and much Alpine thinking to pass the time
when the body was occupied and the mind not. Things had been
arranged in Edinburgh: two girls, Sheila and Rosemarie, from the
University climbing club were going out by car. They wanted
escorts, guides. Smith and I were filling the role. When the money
was made we would go.

By late July we were in the Alps. The abrupt failure of an attempt
to get the girls up the Hörnli Ridge and ourselves up the North Face
of the Matterhorn, combined with very bad weather, sent us rocket-
ing to the Dolomites.

Once again the Tre Cime. Luxury camping and two really good
cooks. The all-pervading evil of the easy life was spreading, and
two days were passed lying in the grass contemplating the walls.
But though we were inactive the master-plan was being hatched.
The fastest time for the route was two days; we reckoned on around
three, considering our slowness on pure aid climbing. We didn't
have a route description, but I knew the start from looking the year
before and then it would be a case of following the fixed pitons.
Here's how the master-plan worked, once we had eliminated that
small difficulty. Somewhere, somehow we had acquired a 300-metre

length of perlon 5-mm. cord. It seemed simple. We would climb
unladen all day. From our high point in the evening the cord would
be lowered to the girls, who'd be waiting on the ground with
sleeping-bags and a precooked hot meal. Up it would come, and
down the remains would go in the morning. What could be more
simple than that?

The morning of the first day's work was cold and dull, and we
overslept. Nine o'clock saw us unwinding the rope at the bottom.
Confidence was way down, only pride kept us going. Neither would
admit to the other that he really wanted to go back to his sleeping-
bag. Anyway, we would have lost face with the girls. Already the
problems of reputations! This time of standing cold at the foot
is often when one forgets great ideals and dedication to climbing,
especially in cold weather. As these dark thoughts were whirling
Robin was off. That was it. Upwards, pessimists!

The climbing was hard and once again our artificial technique was
way out of tune, Scotland then just wasn't the place for artificial
training. The emphasis was too much on free climbing, and we were
lucky if we did 300 feet of artificial a year. Now there was a 600-foot
overhang to contemplate. Slowly a rhythm came. But slow climbing
means the hours pass quickly, and it was already late in the afternoon when I started out on the roof proper. At first it was bewildering: I just couldn't believe the exposure. Space didn't just drop
away beneath your feet as it normally does—my body was tilted
back at forty-five degrees, like, an upside-down crab. Later I was
to do many overhangs, but I'll never forget my introduction on the
Ovest. Somewhere on the previous pitches I had gained confidence,
and I wasn't stumbling any longer. Still slow, yes, but at least
moving smoothly.

Despite the alien climbing and the whirling adjustments in my
head I slowly began to feel happy. It seems ridiculous—to be almost
overcome by a physical feeling of happiness going backwards over
a roof 600 feet above the ground! But there it was. I looked back
towards Robin, impassive as ever. He was whistling a rock-'n-roll
tune on the tiny stance.

Already evening had caught up with us. I reached a hanging
stance on the edge of the roof. There was no doubt about where we
would spend the night: right there, hanging. Robin fumbled up,
muttering in the gloom. About ten feet below he had to stop,

swinging gently in his etriers. There was no room beside me, and no point in both hanging from the same pegs, so we stayed apart.

Now it was time for the master plan to flow smoothly into action. All going well we should be well fed and warm if uncomfortable. Lowering the rope was easy enough; but no sign of the girls below. We shouted down. An English voice answered, but not female. We told him if he saw two girls heading for the Cima Ovest to get them over here, quick. About two hours passed. Cold was creeping in, and we were only in shirts, sweaters and jeans. Contrary to popular belief it can get very cold on the Dolomites at night. Unprintable thoughts about the girls. Suddenly faint voices from the screes: 'Dougal! Robin!'

Faith was restored. There couldn't be much communication as the wind was blowing, but we learnt later that they had been sitting for about three hours beneath the Cima Grande, crying up at the empty overhangs, until they had seen our unknown friend who told them they were at the wrong mountain!

They attached the rucksacks, but this was when the planning went really astray. Have you ever tried hauling a heavy sack straight up through a carabiner for 600 feet? In our ignorance we had never thought of pulleys. Four hours later, with arms sagging weakly, we had the rucksacks. It was now about 2 a.m. An incredible mess of stew and fruit and a thermos of coffee awaited us—but oh, so good! Another hour to get into our sleeping-bags, which can be a difficult movement when you're hanging in etriers.

Climbing should have started at 6 a.m. This hour passed and we were still sleeping deeply. Eventually cramp woke me up around 9 a.m. Merely getting organized took about two hours. We tried to lower the sack down, but the rope became incredibly tangled; Robin tried once or twice to fix it, and when that failed he hurled it off in a rage. Days later we were still picking mangled pieces of Thermos flask and stew out of our sleeping-bags. Now we had to move. No food, no bivouac gear, only some water—I seemed to have done this somewhere before. Some time around noon I moved out of my slings to continue, carrying on in the lead as it would have been too complicated for Robin to pass me.

Fumbling at first, then getting back into a kind of smoothness. Right out onto the edge of the roof and over onto a black blank wall above. A ladder of expansion bolts. Bolts are time-consuming and therefore difficult to place but once they are there it is easy to follow them: that was the theory. Unfortunately, some of these bolts did not seem to like being stuck up on the Ovest overhang, and had tried to get loose. I moved up on two that were stuffed in their holes with paper and wood. Then there was an empty hole before the next one. This could have been serious. We didn't have any bolts, and retreat from there would have been serious to say the least.

I balanced up in the top rung of my etriers. Still too short, and the paper bolt wobbling badly. I couldn't place too much outward strain otherwise it would have been out. Only a downward push was possible. What to do? Robin was still beneath the roof and unaware of what was going on. I tied a short sling to the eye of the bolt. Up again to the top rung, left foot out and into the sling; straighten slowly up. It's really difficult holding balance. Arms slowly round. Above the head and straining with an open carabiner . . . full limit . . . it's there!

It was a good bolt. Faster than I'd moved on the whole climb I clipped everything in, then slumped, drained by nervous tension. That was the end of the dramatics. The rest of the climb was fine. One more cold bivouac on the Kasparek Ledge and we were out early next day. It had been a tough one. Our hands were cut to pieces, heads buzzing. We began to wonder if we could ever plan an organized climb. Or, more worrying, if we did so perhaps it would seem so mundane that we wouldn't enjoy it so much. To many people our innocence and lack of organization may seem almost criminal. But one can have a certain philosophy about it. We were getting out of difficult situations successfully by the strength of our own ability. These wearing experiences were giving us an incredible store for the future. When you have had many epics a normal ascent is that much better an experience, because you know that if the weather turns bad or if things begin to go a little bit wrong you have the knowledge to cope with the emergencies. If you don't have this knowledge the story can have a sad ending. We still had a lot to learn but we were learning.

In 1962 I was back once again amongst the Dolomitic spires, this time with the 'English piton-fancier' Ian Clough as my partner. The year before Ian had climbed the Walker Spur of the Grandes Jorasses and the North Face of the Eiger within a period of ten days.

A quiet, modest Yorkshireman, he made an excellent climbing partner.

For once everything went smoothly: in rapid succession we climbed routes like the Buhlweg on the Roda di Vael, the Aste Diedre on the Crozzondi Brenta and the Oggioni Diedre on the Brenta Alta. That was it: I haven't been back since, as from that time on the Western Alps began to occupy my main thoughts.

CHAPTER FOUR

Eiger

From my early readings the Eiger always had a strong appeal. I have always felt the need for real tests in climbing; basically lazy, I have sometimes turned back on easier routes because I felt they were not testing my capabilities. When I turned to the Alps, the existing route on the North Face seemed to offer a total test of my abilities. At the time there were technically harder routes around but the Eiger seemed to be the most serious of all.

If you are ambitious in climbing and wish to attain top standard in the sport, then it is necessary to tackle progressively a selection of the most difficult climbs around. This progression eventually led me from harder things in Scotland via the hardest things in the Dolomites and Alps to the hardest things in the Himalayas. It is very much a logical movement, each step a necessary part of the whole so that to miss one would leave a bad gap in your mountaineering experience.

This is not a categorical formula for success. One may not have the ability, physical or mental, for this standard of climbing. But the only way to find out is to try. For many people, just one or two parts of the climbing experience are sufficient. There are those who are completely happy climbing in Britain and reach an incredibly high standard in doing so. Similarly, there are those who climb in the Alps and Britain and get up the hardest routes in both countries, but through certain ties—such as jobs, family, lack of ambition, or, on rare occasions, lack of luck—they fail to apply their experience to bigger things. This is not meant as a criticism; I am only trying to explain my attitude to climbing in relation to that of many others. From early days, I found that climbing was the only thing in life that gave me more than momentary satisfaction. Studies and work were always of secondary importance when it came to the

49

mountains. Though around 1963 I still had very vague ideas on the subject, I knew that if I was to give the majority of my life towards climbing it would not be at the level of an instructor in Britain at an outdoor pursuits centre. It would have to be at the top level of the sport, climbing the most difficult climbs and getting completely involved in the historical advance of mountaineering. Otherwise I would quit and try something else. That is my nature.

This may seem to be a digression, but the Eiger played a very important part in the development of my climbing involvement. The mountain itself stands in the Swiss Bernese Oberland, above Grindelwald. Perhaps it's partly because it is so accessible that it has received so much attention: tourists with telescopes can sit in comfort and watch the climbers fighting it out. The ascent of the North Face became one of the great problems of the 1930s: 6,000 feet high, rattling with stones, and notorious for sudden storms. There were a few tragedies. Reactionary alpinists came pouring out of their holes. 'Whoever climbs the Eiger face will have accomplished the most imbecile variant in the history of mountaineering.' And, of course, as the climbers were mostly German: 'Nazis climbing for medals—the glory of the Fatherland.'

I have only contempt for these critics. The climbers were brave people. They climbed, not for glory, but for love of mountains and often as much to get away from Hitler's Germany as to glorify it. The ones who tried the North Face were amongst the best of the time. Accidents happened because the North Face was a very difficult proposition, especially then, with the primitive equipment available. One early tragedy in particular stands out in the memories of all who have had anything to do with the North Face. This was the attempt in 1936 by two Germans, Toni Kurz and Andreas Hinterstoisser, and two Austrians, Edi Rainer and Willy Angerer. Hinterstoisser had found a way across onto the First Icefield by crossing a smooth band of rock on a rope traverse—this means you put in a piton to take the sideways tension on the rope and walk across as far as you can without overbalancing. In case of retreat it would have been advisable to leave a fixed rope in place at this point. Unfortunately the party had to retreat and even more unfortunately they had *not* left a fixed rope. When it came to recrossing the passage—now known as the Hinterstoisser Traverse—they were unable to make it. In their subsequent attempts to abseil down the overhangs beneath in their exhausted state everyone died. Toni Kurz, the last to go, strangled in the rope about thirty feet above the heads of a rescue party; only a knot jammed in a carabiner stood between him and safety, but he was too cold and exhausted to force it through.

It was eventually climbed in 1938 by Heckmaier, Vörg, Kasparek and Harrer, an Austro–German team. Their ascent in four days in bad storm conditions was one of the greatest climbing achievements. By the sixties, when I became interested, the Face had seen around fifty ascents by climbers of many countries. There had been many fatalities, often over-ambitious parties caught out before they were ready to tackle the wall. Heinrich Harrer, a member of the first ascent party has written, in his *The White Spider*, a very informative history of ascents and failures on the Face, which is required reading for anyone interested in the Eiger.

THE SHADOW OF THE EIGER

Summer 1960, and Eley and I were on our way back from the Dolomites. The weather had been wintry, and our only success was the Cassin Route on the West Face of Cima Ovest. A fine climb, but scarcely training for what we were contemplating.

The train arrived at Grindelwald. As it slowed into the station I was still recovering from the biggest shock of my climbing life. I'd read everything that had been written about the North Face of the Eiger, but I was still unprepared for the sheer size of the face that dominated the Grindelwald valley. We didn't speak but I could see Eley was feeling the same. What were we in for?

The route was easy to pick out, as I had the diagram from *The White Spider* in memory. The long, easy-angled tower section leading up to the Difficult Crack and the Hinterstoisser Traverse. The First and Second Icefields, linked by the frozen tunnel of the Ice Hose. Up from the end of the Second Icefield to the Flatiron was a rock spur, with the Death Bivouac on its summit, where the first two climbers to attempt the Face—Max Sedlmayer and Karl Mehringer in 1935—had perished after a very bold and courageous attempt. Then the traverse of the Third Icefield to the long gully of the Ramp, and the exit ledge from this called the Traverse of the Gods. This crossing took one into the Fourth Icefield, known as the White

Spider because of the tentacles of ice spreading out from its lower rim. Out of the Spider into the Exit Cracks, and then where every candidate wanted to get to—the Summit Icefield leading to the Mitellegi Ridge and finally the summit.

On up the path to Alpiglen. Into the hotel and a big surprise: there were four other British climbers there, one of whom we knew well, Geoff Oliver from Newcastle. It was obvious they weren't there to pick edelweiss so we came straight to the point. Geoff was having trouble with his team, two of whom had no heart for the North Face, so we reckoned on teaming up two ropes of two, Eley with me and Geoff with Dennis English.

The next day we made a reconnaissance, climbing about a thousand feet up the easy lower section of the Face. Initial impressions were not very good: bad rock, rubble-covered ledges, waterfalls and uninteresting climbing. But we knew all this from the books. This section was usually climbed in the early morning or late afternoon, depending on where you wanted to bivouac or how you wanted to tackle the Face. For our attempt we chose to start in the afternoon and bivouac beneath the Difficult Crack, which is the first of the real pitches.

The afternoon passed, climbing steadily up the rubbish, and we established a bivvy just beneath the Crack. As we were sitting comfortably in our tent sacks there was suddenly a loud explosion and a great hissing all around. We were not to be spared the typical Eiger storm, creeping in innocently on a cloud, saving everything to drop on the wall. Soon we were covered in flashing cloud and hailstones. A long, miserable night, then stumbling wetly downwards in the morning. The Face was completely white. We didn't renew our attempt. I wasn't too keen: something inside told me I wasn't yet experienced enough for the North Wall. In retrospect, the storm was a good thing. It gave me an insight into the problems of the Eiger, and also probably kept us all from making fools of ourselves. To be sure we might have got up; but if there had been a big storm high up on the Face, I think we might have lacked the experience to pull through to a successful conclusion.

FIRST REFUSAL

Though we'd been rejected, the Eiger was still there. I read and re-read *The White Spider*. Then, in 1961, the German–Austrian team of Hiebeler, Kinshofer, Mannhardt and Almberger made the first winter ascent. This turned climbing circles upside down. Few climbs had been attempted in the Alpine winter and to complete one of the hardest was a great feat. I didn't think of emulating that, but kept on thinking about getting up in summer. There was now a lot of thought about the Face in British climbing circles. Parties from Britain had climbed most of the other existing hard routes in the Alps, but the most famous of all was still awaiting its first British ascent. Chris Bonington and Don Whillans had been active the previous year, but had been turned back repeatedly by bad weather.

During the winter of 1962, Robin and I planned to go on the Face together. He was going on a British Expedition to the Pamirs, so would be super-fit on his return to the Alps. I was going on expedition to the canning factories of Kent but hoped to put in two or three Alpine weeks before Robin got back.

I was working the night shift to make more money. Stumbling out one bright clear Kentish morning I made my way to the paper shop as usual. Peering uninterestedly at the headlines I saw: *Disaster in Pamirs. British climbers fall to their death.* A great numbness came over me. I read on. It was the worst: Robin had fallen on the descent from Pic Garmo with Wilfred Noyce. It was the first time I'd come to the death of someone I knew well, and it just seemed so strange that I'd never see him again. So distant and far away. Years of memories that were now only for me, never again to be discussed over a pint. The cause of the accident was never known. They were descending a snow slope roped together; someone slipped; both went down. At the time there were many suppositions and attempts to pin the fault on one of the two. Why trouble? They were both dead.

It was a bad summer for picking up the newspaper. I'd just arranged to team up with Andy Wightman, who was also working in the pea-fields, when there was another series of headlines. *British climbers in trouble on the Eiger . . . British climber falls to his death . . . Dramatic rescue on Eiger.*

This was an attempt by Brian Nally and Barry Brewster, which had ended when Brewster had been hit by a stone on the Flatiron. He had fallen onto the Second Icefield, breaking his back in the process. Nally had made him comfortable during the night and next morning had set off for help. Just as he started to cross the Second

Icefield another volley of stones swept Brewster from the Face.
Deeply shocked, Nally was taken in tow and brought down by
Chris Bonington and Don Whillans, who had been in the process of
making yet another attempt.

The beginning of August saw us in Grindelwald, after being chased
from the North Face of the Matterhorn yet again by bad conditions.
It would have been wiser to attempt a training route, but the Eiger
was so large in our minds that we felt we could not give enough
concentration to a lesser climb—a thing that can be fatal. Often
when one has a major object in mind and decides to do a lesser as
training, one forgets that the training route can also be a hard and
serious climb and goes into it without full concentration. I have
often been slapped violently out of ultra-relaxed climbing on this
type of route and forced into using every skill I possess. But this
time we decided that our overall fitness was adequate and that we'd
concentrate everything on the one objective.

The time felt right. Other climbers were on the Face, and there
had already been one or two successful teams. We could not
justifiably put it off any longer. It is very easy to sit at the foot of
the Eiger in relaxing sun seeing it get bigger and feeling your will
power grow weaker. I knew this insidious feeling from previous
waiting periods. This time we spent one night at Alpiglen and moved
onto the Face the next afternoon. I had the best equipment I'd
possessed up until now: new boots, a new down jacket and tent sack.
We even had miners' helmets to protect us from the notorious
Eiger stonefall. The Face is very loose, and there is a constant pitter-
patter of stonefall, but when the sun hits the upper icefield and rocks
all hell seems to break loose. Melting snow causes streams and
waterfalls which loosen the rocks, and on certain parts of the Face
at certain times it is impossible to climb because of this. Many of the
accidents on the Face have been caused simply by people being in
the wrong place at the wrong time.

The sacks seemed heavy as we moved up the rubbly start, which
I remembered well from my previous attempt. Our plan was roughly
the same: bivouac beneath the Difficult Crack, then as far as possible
the next day. A good night and fine morning gave us no excuses.
Over the famous passages. The wall seemed in good condition. Andy
led the Difficult Crack; I danced over a perfectly dry Hinterstoisser
Traverse. There was an old rope which I barely used—the Traverse

could certainly be climbed free in similar conditions. Onward, speeding upward, to be brought to a halt by the slabs between the First and Second Icefields. Difficult climbing, no protection and time-consuming, but eventually we were on the Second Icefield.

Here a bad mistake in planning came to light. The icefield was bare, hard, black water ice. We had blunt crampons. There was no alternative but to cut steps. We had envisaged ourselves dancing across the icefields on front points, but here we were hacking never-endingly the staircase of our own bad planning. It was 3 o'clock in the afternoon when we reached the upper rim of the icefield, glad to be temporarily out of reach of the perpetual patter of pebbles. All the timing was going wrong. Crossing the Flatiron was a tense experience: loose rock, waterfalls and stonefall. At 7 we were glad to prepare a bivouac site on the Flatiron.

We had hoped to stop in the Ramp that night, but looking across I could see this would have been difficult even if we had managed to get there. There was a party of eight very slow Italians ahead of us, trying to make the first Italian ascent, and across on the Ramp one could hear babbling Latin voices from every ledge and hole. Interesting thoughts about how to get past them on the morrow. It's usually straightforward to pass a rope of two, but getting past eight would be an enormous problem. Food for thought—and also, thinking about food, we did not have enough for three more bivouacs and it looked as if it would take the Italians at least that to get up the wall.

Cooking was just finished when there was a violent rush of hail-stones on the tent sack. While we had been brewing and contemplating, another Eiger storm had whipped in. This time it was no small one. All night it beat upon us. There could be only one decision in the morning—descent. That was a long way but it would be even worse going slowly upwards. The Italians were now committed to fighting their way out.

Good luck, we thought, abseiling down the waterfall which was the flank of the Flatiron. The Second Icefield was horrendous. We cowered and huddled on the upper rim as the water, ice and rocks shot out over the protective bulge. Protection was fine for the Traverse, but we knew that sometime we'd have to quit safety and make at least three abseils down the icefield to reach the rocks beside the Ice Hose. The Traverse was uneventful; we were soaked but warm with continuous movement. Eventually the bad moment came. Shoulders hunched, hard hat firm, rucksack high like a shield, I slowly abseiled out onto the icefield. The stonefall had fortunately slackened to a small pitter-patter but the volume of water was incredible. On our way up we'd wondered about the many deep grooves worn in the ice: now we knew. They were regular river-beds in the storms.

I had stopped to place an ice-piton for the next abseil when there was a great banging about a hundred feet to the left. A shifty glance from beneath the rim of my crash hat revealed a huge slab of rock, bouncing and shattering with a terrible acrid smell down the icefield. I suppose being in a stonefall area is the nearest thing we war babies and non-combatants can come to experiencing shell-fire. It is the feeling of utter hopelessness that prevails. There were no safer alternative routes: the stones could come any time—anywhere. There was no point in even being afraid. There had to be a straight, unemotional acceptance, with the mind continuously alert for evasive action if that is possible. This time nothing happened to us and we reached the shelter of the Swallow's Nest intact.

The reversing of the Hinterstoisser Traverse was not easy. Soaked again, and skidding on the stretched old rope. We did not known at this time that Whillans had discovered an abseil from above which completely avoided the whole traverse: if this had been known in the early days, the whole Toni Kurz disaster could have been avoided. Unroped, we continued downward. A quick abseil over the Difficult Crack. Now there was nothing but 1,500 feet of loose wandering to the bottom. On this section one occasionally meets small bulging sections between ledges. Each in his separate daze wandered down a succession of these. Suddenly I heard a muffled shout. I'd just come over one of these little overhangs and was standing on a ledge. I glanced over to my left and there was Andy falling. He hit the ledge, then bounced and began rolling. I thought: Christ, he'll never stop, and it's still a thousand feet to the bottom! Scrabbling mightily with his hands he came to a halt about 150 ft. below. I quickly rushed downward, but as I was climbing another strange sight materialized: two climbers in yellow, shouting in Italian, traversing from the left also towards Andy. No one said much as we reached him. Everyone was too involved in what the damage would be. He didn't look too nice, blood streaming down his face, but he was obviously not too bad as a steady coherent, swearing bout was proving. 'I've broken my bloody ankle.'

Sure enough one ankle was hanging loose and twisted badly. The head cut, though wide, was superficial. The rim of his hard hat had pushed forward and sliced open his face over the cheekbone. Gory but not immobilizing. But what to do? Thoughts of soloing down and alerting a rescue party, but that would have meant a major operation. Brain-racking, I re-read my *White Spider* mentally. It clicked: the Gallery Window! This was the waste-shaft from the Eiger–Jungfrau railway which came out onto the Face below and to the right of the Difficult Crack. We must be very near it. It was the traditional escape for hard-pressed parties escaping from the Face, and it was from here that the rescue-party had so nearly reached Toni Kurz. I think this was in the Italians' minds as well, and we tried various phrases in different languages. A basic French was the only one to work. That at least was something. I learnt that they were Nando Nusdeo from Milan and Luigi Alippi from Lecco. They had been preparing their bivouac when Andy had come tumbling out of the clouds. Being good Catholics they thought it was some kind of divine apparition until they saw the climbing equipment and the blood.

Andy was in pain but bearing it well. A plan was worked out. By fortune in misfortune we were only about 150 feet beneath the Gallery Window. Sign language and pidgin French produced a scheme: the Italians would climb up to the window and throw down a couple of ropes, and I would attempt to climb up with Andy on my back. By this time it was dark and it seemed to take ages before we could start. Andy was stubbornly insisting he could hop, but we worked out a compromise whereby he sat on my shoulders and used his hands while I provided the legs—it is difficult to look upwards with someone on your shoulders. A kind of two-man man.

Ages of long hard sweating saw us collapsing into the tunnel. It was an incredibly strange sensation of contrast. In fact the tunnel is a very weird place. Out of the wild blowing rain of the Nordwand into an electrically lit science-fiction cave with eerie, moaning winds. To add to the sense of the ridiculous there was a neon advertisement by the entrance. I could only stand shaking my head in bewilderment. It was almost too much for my mind, which was still grappling with the day's retreat and the accident.

It was warmer inside the tunnel but still cold. Andy was now beginning to look shocked and shivering. Eigerwand station was about an hour's walk uphill, and there we hoped to find an office and maybe some heat to cook hot drinks. That hour was one of the longest of my life. It was about three in the morning, and I'd been going for nearly twenty-three hours. We took turns at carrying Andy. This produced a strange effect for me: I felt so exhausted when I took my turn that I thought I'd fall down, but upon beginning to move it was almost like breaking through a barrier and coming out fresh on the other side. A dream state, where my mind closed but my legs kept moving. Every time it was my turn to rest, the exhaustion came pouring back and I sagged against the wall. Then the station was there, with electric stove and blankets. Exhausted sleep till the first train and the sightseers and questions and despondent descent to the newspapers and hospital.

Andy recovered in Interlaken. I was so depressed I went back to Scotland. Later that summer Chris Bonington and Ian Clough made the first British ascent of the North Face of the Eiger.

ALL THINGS COME . . .

By now my involvement with the Eiger was total. I reached the foot of it at the end of July 1963 as fit as I've ever been, after a prolonged session in the Dolomites and an ascent in bad conditions of the North Face of the Plan in Chamonix. My partner was twenty-two-year-old Rusty Baillie, a strong Rhodesian climber who'd settled in Britain as an instructor. We'd done some climbing in Scotland and he'd been with me on the Plan, so the stage was set for another go. Rusty, powerfully built and red-haired with an open, cheerful lace, was an easy companion, and I felt relaxed and confident as we wandered slowly through the grassy meadows, passing the odd peacefully munching cow. It made everything seem slightly incongruous. Most Alpine walls are reached by glaciers and moraines, but to start on the most feared of all you step off the pastures onto the rock.

I've always favoured the afternoon approach on the Eiger. Most people tended to start at midnight and climb as high as possible but I preferred a slower introduction. The easy afternoon wander with heavy packs gives my mind time to adjust to the variety of enormous problems it will have to cope with in the days ahead. Rusty was there a few paces behind, also engrossed in his thoughts. This year we were early. There had been no ascents. Probably a few icy pitches awaited us. No matter: we felt confident in our fitness and ability.

Slowly the afternoon passed away to the tinkle of cowbells and regular motion over the rubble-coated ledges. Slightly bored in the late afternoon, we stopped in a cave to the left of the Gallery Window. Memories of the year before. How would it end this time?

The night mists closed in as duvets were sought. The Face is an eerie place at that time. Clouds coming and going and the odd rock falling and terra firma calling with a lonely alpenhorn from Kleine Scheidegg. I know where we both wanted to be.

But it wasn't to be. The Monday was cold and frosty, so no excuses. Just as we moved into the shadowy dawn, two other climbers appeared, Max Friedwager and Friedl Schicker from Salzburg. They seemed competent enough on this ground. Onward, still warming, to the Difficult Crack. More shocks. The wall was dry all right but the rock was hidden by the Eiger's secret weapon: verglas, a thin film of ice on the rock. Rusty led, tiptoeing on the clear spots. A little test, but chicken feed compared with what we subsequently had to climb. A constant process of adaptation this. Harder all the time. Not to worry. The sky was blue. What was a Scottish winter training for anyway?

Over the Hinterstoisser and into the front line. Not much artillery as yet, just little pebble hits. But what's this? Rusty's talking to someone. The first descent? Front line madness? Talking to himself? No. It was Walter Bonatti, an Italian, one of the best post-war climbers, trudging valleywards after a night of over-enthusiastic stonefall which had put an end to his attempt at the first solo. He seemed happy enough but he was off down. Onward went the idiots. The big pitch between the icefields was hard, the next still a bit tenuous, and the Ice Hose bypass really far out. The hose itself was untouchable—a huge boss of green water ice. The Austrians were still in front here and this was where we found they could climb—and well. The pitch was a 150-foot run-out over verglas-covered slabs. No pitons, and odd attempts to put one in only resulted in hitting a dead end after a quarter of an inch. Friedl, on his lead, managed it muttering, but skilfully all the same. To keep up the Scottish end I had to appear calm and whistled 'I Like It'. That's not how I felt. But it gave in and we charged on to the Second

Icefield with hopes of lovely snow ice. No peace for the wicked, though: black, stone-scarred water ice. Memories of crampon runs receded.

A nasty business, this. A little run. Front points thrusting, hand-spike stabbing. Can't take much of it though. It was a step every few feet. Max took the first run-out and fixed a rope to an ice-peg. We ran up the hand-rail and thrust through into the lead. This process was repeated until we reached the upper rim. Hardly pure climbing, one might say, but purism is for the valleys; the Second Icefield is not the place for a discussion on climbing ethics.

At the upper rim, we were hungry, but rest was not on the menu. The Flatiron had to be reached before 5 p.m. otherwise it would be a too-low bivouac or probably a ride down to Grindelwald on the back of a rock. We crossed the icefield in two hours, which is normal fast time; it was the eggshell tiptoes between the icefields that had consumed the hours. Speed was improving, however, and we reached the safety of the Death Bivouac just as the sun hit the top of the wall and the Spider started spewing all hell down the sides of the Flatiron. Poor Max however got caught in a waterfall, but they don't break bones. There was still time to push on, but nowhere to go: the Third Icefield was like a battlefield. So it was out with the duvets and stoves and a long session of brewing loomed up. It was a reasonable bivouac site. Sleep was sought and not attained; there was enough warmth but no room. We kept twanging onto the ropes.

It got very cold towards dawn as the sun started on its shift again—nice to look at but still two climbing days away. However, we imagined we were warm, and by seven I wasn't imagining any more as I headed out onto the dream-chasing baldness of the Third Icefield. The Eiger said hello with a rock. I wasn't feeling sociable so thumped a big ice-peg into its glassy innards. A bit unsporting to send a brick so early.

The hand-rail was fixed again and Max came front-pointing and tension traversing through to the foot of the ramp. Two twos again, and swift progress as well. Off with the crampons. Feel like a fairy. Up we go. Three pitches in all. But what's this? A beautiful sight loomed up: yellow overhanging walls with a shimmering green icicle between. Aesthetically incredible. There was only one thing wrong—we had to climb it. So this was the famous waterfall pitch. Max shook his head and said he would try the variation on the right. But this looked just as bad: rotten yellow rock, loose pegs and old retreat slings hanging near the top. We knew that people had been misled here before, and preferred to tackle the waterfall.

So commenced a rough session for me. It looked hard and was. The pegs were hidden under a great bulge of ice—the walls of the chimney covered with verglas. It was a long series of front-point wriggles. The exit took the lot—right crampon off, left one on, a pull, and a leftover expansion bolt in sight. Two more moves and I was twisting and shouting in a great release of nervous tension. Rusty hastened up and through on a still hard-looking pitch. There was still only the odd grunt from Max; he seemed to be having trouble. As yet no cries for a rope, so I whipped up and almost fell off with fright at the sight of the ice bulge. Ice, ice and more bloody ice. But it had to be done so I launched upwards on scraping, now blunt crampons. The bulge wasn't so bad as it looked. Straightforward ice hacking. What an exit, though!

It looked easy enough. Only ten feet of slab between me and the Upper Ramp icefield. I didn't like that ten feet. Holds tend to get smaller and slabs smoother as one reminisces, but there really weren't any holds. One nick in the verglas was scraped, and I studied form for a long time before venturing a front left crampon point onto it. Teetering slightly, I dropped the axe onto the slab to make another scrape—I couldn't swing it, as any violent movement would have removed the point from its niche. This was repeated four times before I could at last grovel in the snow. Now that confidence was really building up, as it was only midday and I knew that only a weather break would stop us. Summit visions sprang to mind and I started singing and shouting.

I was still doing it two hours later as Rusty was trying to dangle a line to some Austrian bait beneath an overhang. Max had stuck at the top of the bypass pitch and standing in an etrier had brought Friedl up to stand on his head. Even then they couldn't make it, so we dropped a rope. But they had trouble getting out due to their precarious position. At last Max got a grip and managed to swarm up the rope to Rusty and then to me. Great hand-shakings, but the summit was lost for the day as we didn't think the Spider would be in an amiable mood at about four in the afternoon. More trouble came in the shape of the Brittle Ledge. Like climbing on a coal tip! Then on with the tour and up a fine crack to the well-named

Traverse of the Gods. What a ledge this is! Only Grade 3, but 4,000 sobering feet on your right keeps the delight within bounds. Orgies of photo-taking ensued as we meandered to the end of the traverse. What a wall—4,500 of vertical and 10,500 of actual climbing done, and still a hard 1,500 to come. As we sat brewing up on our ledge, the feeling of being really small crept over. Alone in a vast acreage of rock. Nowhere to go but up, and the up part a heaving, spewing mass of rock and ice. We prayed hard for a cold night and tried to sleep. More amusement with Max making a functional sacrifice on the end of a rope. Then their petrol stove blew up and sent them scurrying out of their tent sack helpless with laughter. We were still enjoying the whole experience.

Max's sacrifice must have been acceptable as it was a fine, bitterly cold morning. Tough on the telescopes though: Grindelwald was shrouded in valley cloud. Up the Spider tiptoed the crampon-pointed flies. It was on with the old game of run-teeter-and-hack on the glassy water ice. The exit cracks loomed up. No easy passage this year. Verglas-coated tentacles waiting for the puny Spider-bait. Max was champing at the bit after yesterday's little failure and led a vicious pitch at the start of the cracks. I gladly took a pull on the rope. It was really cold and any waiting at all made one sluggish. Then, wonder of wonders, two more climbers appeared on the Spider. Friendly greetings and thoughts that they were making fast time. The reason became apparent when the leader approached and thanked us for our steps on the icefields. It had been freezing so hard that our steps had remained intact and they'd rocketed up climbing together. The leader of this Swiss team was Erich Friedli, one of the best climbers ever to come out of that country, but another who did not live to fulfil his youthful promise. He was killed a year later while trying a winter ascent on the North Face of the Gletscherhorn in the Oberland. They were fresher and faster, so we let them through.

Another famous pitch ahead—the white quartz crack. This had been the scene of many epics of the past. It was here in 1952 that Buhl pulled an international rope of Germans, French and Austrians through to safety with a fantastic effort, and here that in 1962 four exposure-crazy Swiss had to be roped up by an Austrian party. My lead again. A pleasant surprise this time. Still plenty of verglas but nothing like as hard as the pitches on the Ramp or between the icefields. An enjoyable piece of work. Then scenes of more past epics as Corti's bivouac site loomed up.

Claudio Corti and Stefano Longhi had been attempting to make the first Italian ascent of the Face in 1957. They had met two German climbers Günter Waltdurft and Franz Mayr on the lower part and teamed up into a rope of four. Their progress had been very slow. Eventually Longhi fell when they took a false traverse line out of the Ramp and above the Traverse of the Gods. He finished beneath an overhang and they'd been unable to get him up, so had left him and tried to climb out to get help. Corti took a bad fall in the exit cracks, so the Germans made him in turn comfortable and tried to climb out for help. They succeeded in climbing out but were swept down and killed in an avalanche on the West Flank descent route. Meanwhile a rescue team had reached the summit with a winch and steel cable. By lowering a German rescue expert, Alfred Hillepart from Munich, they had been able to winch Corti out on his back, but bad weather had prevented a rescue of Longhi and he'd died on his lonely stance. We looked up and shuddered. A tremendous act of courage to enter into this rattling mass of wall on a thin wire thread.

A short tension traverse, then into a long crack. Reports of many pitons sprang to mind, but they were buried in the ice-choked bed. A slightly worrying long run-out followed until an old ring-peg was reached. Slowly the wall was easing. But it would be unlike the Eiger to give up without a final struggle. There it was ahead, the sting in the tail, the Summit Icefield. Specially prepared for the unwary. The tension is easing and one tends to relax, but the mind must wind up the crampon muscles for a last grinding 300 feet.

It was in bad condition as well. We were now in the sun, but though welcoming the warmth were also slightly unhappy as it had melted the icefield's outer cover. Mushy ice caused us to move very carefully up to the summit ridge, with the thought always in mind of the Swiss team, Wyss and Gonda, who had come through the whole wall and fallen from this icefield: if ever the Eiger played a dirty trick that was one. The last stretches of the Mittellegi Ridge and the summit was there. It was good to relax again even though temporarily. But hunger soon drove us down the rotten West Ridge slabs to the delights of a bed and bath in the Scheidegg Hotel, by courtesy of the Press.

CHAPTER FIVE

The Western Alps

After the Eiger I was in a quandary for a little while. I wanted to get into winter Alpine climbing but did not know enough about it, or anyone who could tell me what to do. I also wanted to try some new routes in summer but again didn't have much information. By new routes I don't mean small fill-in lines but major climbs.

Partners were also a problem. I had outgrown all my early companions. Moriarty, Stenhouse and Wightman were virtually retired; the Marshalls climbed only occasionally in Scotland; Rusty had gone back to Rhodesia. Consequently I was doing most of my climbing with Joy Heron. This was fine in Scotland and for lesser things in the Alps, as she was as good as any woman climber in Britain, but for bigger things she lacked the necessary stamina and experience.

Joy and I were in the Chamonix camp site that year and managed to fit in a few training climbs such as the Moine and the Salbitschen before the hordes arrived. A chance encounter with a London climber, Grant 'Jug' Jarvis, led to the second ascent of the North Face of the Pointe Migot, which had been climbed a few days previously by Chris Bonington, Tom Patey, Joe Brown and Robin Ford. After this I wanted to do one of the routes on the Dru, but Jug had already climbed the West Face so I was footloose again. But Jug, being a friendly guy, introduced me to a London friend of his, Bev Clark. Bev had just fallen out with his climbing partner and was also looking for someone to climb with. Jug recommended him. The four of us, Joy, Jug, Bev and I, did the South Ridge of the Pèlerins. That seemed O.K., Bev could climb, so two days later he and I were bivouacked beneath the West Face of the Dru. We talked about previous climbs and experiences.

64

The West Face of the Dru at that time was Bev's greatest ambition. There was a lot of aid climbing on this route and he assured me he had done plenty of this. It was only when we got to the start of the difficulties the next morning that I found out it was the first time he had ever used etriers. At first I was flabbergasted, but I had been reckoning on leading the climb anyway so decided to push on and hope that he'd learn fast. In fact he learnt quickly, and except for turning upside down at the Bloque Coincé, an A3 overhang, he was moving really well by the end of the climb.

This is a beautiful face, but in 1964 it was already spoilt by an excess of rusty pitons and rotten wooden wedges. I would have loved it initially. What a great line! It seems fair to leave pitons in place in the Dolomites, as continual nailing and de-nailing would destroy the limestone, but in the solid granite of Chamonix there is no excuse. This over-pitoning drags a route like the West Face, the Bonatti Pillar or the East Face of the Capucin down to the level of climbers who would not have been able to tackle it in its virgin state. It means 'over-population, lessening of standards and obvious rock dangers from having lots of clumsy boots kicking around.

Bev and I completed our ascent uneventfully, and I was so impressed with his performance that I asked him if he wanted to do the Walker Spur on the North Face of the Grandes Jorasses with me. He immediately said yes, and we began planning on the walk down to Montenvers. It seemed simple enough: two days' rest then back up to the Leschaux hut. But simple plans never seem to work out simply. On that day came a meeting that was to change my climbing life.

They were just in the process of building the Mont Blanc tunnel, and the subsidized workers' cafeteria was open to the public. It was as cheap to eat there as to buy food and cook it, so every night it was filled with the residents of the Biolay camp-site.

Bev, Joy and I were celebrating the Dru when the athletic figure of John Harlin, an American climber, came across to the table. Bev and he were friends from a meeting in Wales. He had a good reputation—new routes on the South Face of the Fou and the Hidden Pillar of Frêney, Eiger North Face and a fast winter ascent of the Eiger's neighbour, the Mönch Nordwand. We shook hands and sat sizing each other up, neither of us being prone to verbosity. Bev kept the conversation going as only he can. Then there was a silence, broken only by the munching of horse steaks. John suddenly broke the pause, addressing himself to me.

'I'd like to try the Shroud on the Jorasses and I'd also like to have you along. How do you feel?'

That was typical of John as I was later to find out. No nonsense. Straight to the point if he really wanted something.

I looked at Bev. My promises were to him, yet he seemed to know that this was something I couldn't refuse. It was a possible step in the direction I wanted to take.

The Shroud was an unclimbed, very steep 3,000-foot icefield to the left of the Walker Spur—it had already repulsed efforts by several well known climbers. With John I knew that I would have a sufficiently hardened companion. All these thoughts flashed through my head in seconds. 'You're on.' Thereafter conversation turned to planning. We'd move up to the Leschaux hut the next day; the weather forecast was good. Bev would come up and carry some supplies for us.

We arrived in the late afternoon, heavily laden; everything looked good. Weather was fine, conditions good, but later on John suddenly felt feverish and began to vomit. It continued through the night, so we decided to wait a day to see if it would clear up. The next day, though frustrating, was highly interesting. It was like an international meet at the Leschaux, with some of the best European climbers of the day buzzing around. Walter Bonatti turned up, waiting for Michel Vaucher to join him for a new route on the Pointe Whymper. Michel arrived with his wife Yvette and a friend, who were going to try the Walker. In the evening came Pierre Mazeaud and Roberto Sorgato, also for the Walker. With the odd German thrown in it was real hustle and bustle.

During the morning I had wandered across to have a look at the approach to the Shroud. As I was leaving the hut two figures passed on the Glacier below, going at high speed. I followed about half an hour behind. It was too early for anyone to be thinking of bivouacking on the lower rocks of the Walker. Where were they heading? Soon there was no doubt. Keeping steadily leftward they stopped at the foot of the Shroud. Competition, and French voices. They started to rope up and put on their hard hats. Suddenly there was a great rumbling and a shower of stones came volleying down the

Shroud. They ran for cover but there was none. I saw a large rock splinter hit the hard hat of one of the Frenchmen.

Christ, I thought, he's in trouble!

But he must have had a good hard hat, or a tough head. A few minutes later he was standing cursing and shaking his head. But there seemed to be sense in that head. Half an hour later they had repacked rucksacks and were heading off down the glacier again. I hid in a crevasse as they passed. We later learnt that they were the French climbers Desmaison and Bertrand, who'd heard we were going to try the Shroud and had rushed to get on to it first.

Returning to the hut I found John noticeably better. We'd start on the morrow. At 2 a.m. whisperings and clattering of boots: the Walker parties disappear. Decision to wait ten minutes. Both of us asleep again . . . . Four o'clock! God, we're late! A hasty cup of tea and off into the night. The lower rocks of the Walker were like Blackpool tower, climbers' head-lamps winking everywhere; further to the right we could see two small pinpricks on the Whymper icefield.

It was daylight before we started. In view of the experiences of our rivals, we started up the rocks to the right of the Shroud. Fairly straightforward climbing, but slowed by the size of our packs. After 500 feet of this we hit the Shroud proper. It was steep all right—65° or more, and all ice. We decided to climb on the extreme right, glove-jamming in the crack between rock and ice and laybacking up the edge. No step-cutting, so we really moved. By late afternoon we were over half-way. A bivouac site was the only problem; there was nothing on the icefield. John climbed about a rope's length up the buttress and found an overhang with a ledge underneath. We felt elated; the water was boiling and the compliments were flowing. Our first climb, and teamwork working really well. Both climbing safely at high standard, because it had been hard climbing. But some time during the night John peered out of the tent sack.

'Hell, the weather's changing.'

Sure enough, the air was warmer and stars were being blotted out in the west. In the morning it was still fine though clouds were building. An abseil dumped us back on the Shroud. Up or down? The ice at this point got really steep. John led an artificial pitch; I followed and went through. Far-out climbing. I'd gone about fifty feet when a black cloud came sweeping in over the summit of the Jorasses and dropped its load right on us. Huge hailstones, almost as painful as small rocks. There was no question of what to do. I rattled back to John and the retreat began.

It was important to get off the icefield quickly. It was a natural chute: everything from the upper part would be channelled down it. After about six abseils we decided to abandon the Shroud and make the long traverse to the Walker Spur. On this traverse came one of the most helpless moments of my climbing career. I was belaying John. He was about fifty feet away when there was an incredible flash and lightning struck the rock between us. An ultraviolent thunderclap left us deafened and dazed. The seconds passed. Would it strike again? Slowly as we recovered perspective the core of the storm passed and moved on to other pastures. It was an incredible feeling, just waiting for the strike knowing there was nothing to do, nowhere to go. The rest of the descent was normal. Completely sodden, we reached the hut just after dark.

Vaucher and Bonatti had to climb for two more days before getting out—still in the storm. They'd reckoned it easier up than down, especially as their rope had been cut in three places by heavy stonefall.

But John and I were happy even in defeat. We'd found that we were very compatible on the mountain, and seemed to make a good team. That storm virtually ended the summer. Already on the way down we were making plans to climb together in the winter.

Alpine Winter Fumblings

Winter 1965—I had given up everything so I could have a season in the Alps. Three months' work in London had provided the wherewithal for a frugal existence. I didn't care about the frugality: at last I was getting a chance to spend a long time in the winter Alps, and in the company of a man who had already done major winter ascents.

John Harlin had a concrete room in the basement of his Leysin chalet. Have you ever tried living with concrete all around at minus temperatures? My first move was to 'borrow' a stove from one of the disused summer chalets—it smoked badly but I preferred watery eyes to a frozen body. Food was leftovers from the family meals at the American school where John was sports director—'sports' being climbing and skiing.

To go anywhere in the winter you have to be able to ski, so I had borrowed a pair of shorty skis from Grahame Tiso. These I got around on, but the techniques learnt caused irreparable damage to my future skiing style. As I couldn't afford lift tickets, walking up and skiing down strengthened the legs. A friendly lift attendant started to give me tickets, and my standard began to improve, but unfortunately he was absent the day I went without a ticket and I had to leave for the woods in a great hurry. After about two weeks of skiing and training in the low quarries, John suggested that we should do a winter ascent.

The proposed climb was the North Face of the Tour d'Ai, 900 feet, a Grade 6 that John had done in summer, which awaited both its second and its first winter ascent.

A late start as usual. You have to take two lifts to get to within about ten minutes of the start. There were two starts, a 150-foot aid pitch or the same length of free Grade 6 corner. We were two ropes of two: John with Bob Boucher, myself with Ted Wilson. John and Ted were American climbing instructors working as assistants under John Harlin. Being the visitor, I was given the choice; being Scottish, I chose the free pitch.

Christ, it was cold. Four hours later I was almost regretting my choosing. Hard climbing, fingers freezing, and stupid me had climbed it with a rucksack. Boucher got up just before dark on the other pitch, so John and he decided to quit and go down to Leysin. I didn't fancy the ski descent so tried to persuade Ted, when he came up, to bivouac and finish the climb next day. But he would have none of it: he wanted his wife and his warm apartment. I thought of my concrete basement and the descent again, and became even more persuasive. No go. Abseiling into the dark we left a fixed rope for a future attempt. The descent was every bit the nightmare I had imagined.

I wanted to get back as quickly as possible but the others were all ski instructing. At last about four days later I caught Bob Boucher in a weak moment and persuaded him to go again. With the hardest pitch done, we reckoned it would go fairly quickly, so we left all the bivouac gear behind except for a down jacket and launched upwards again. Surprise, surprise. Here for the first time I learnt to distrust John's memory. He'd remembered climbing at about Grade 5 on the second pitch, but I found myself struggling with a loose A2 wall, beating pins into frozen turf. There were two pitches like that, then at last a long, easyish free one that Bob led. That took us into a cave. We got there the same time as the dark.

It was as cold as a January night in the Alps can be. Down jackets and a bar of chocolate were certainly not enough to keep the outside temperature from getting at our inner cores. Five o'clock dark and seven o'clock light: for fourteen hours we froze. I did not warm up until I'd clumsily blundered up the last pitch in the morning. Even then we weren't finished. It took us five hours in powder snow and one abseil to get off the Tour d'Ai. Sitting afterwards in the café, I began to reflect on the difficulties of Alpine winter climbing. It was vastly different from Scotland. We were only in the low Alps, but the temperatures even here were much colder. Instead of tackling gullies or buttresses with a good covering of climbable ice, one was faced with acres of unconsolidated powder snow on rock—sometimes with verglas. The approaches were much more difficult and so too were the descents. All in all, it looked like a hard business. But this made me want all the more to get involved with it—so involved that the next project was a trip to Kleine Scheidegg to examine the possibilities of a true direct route on the Eiger North Face.

CHAPTER SIX

Eiger Direct

Most of the parties who climb the Eiger come down saying, 'A magnificent experience—but never again.' I could not quite understand this. To be sure, it is unusual for a climber to repeat a major route; it is a thing completed and there are so many new things to do. But the statement was not relating only to this feeling. It was saying something about the whole North Face of the Eiger itself. Climbers seemed to experience a great sense of relief when finishing the North Face. The psychological impact of that great wall and its history has been so great that potential climbers seemed to be conditioned to the idea that they were going into a disaster area. This is not an unreasonable feeling: the wall *is* dangerous. But there again, accepting danger and trying to minimize it with one's experience is an essential part of climbing.

On reaching Kleine Scheidegg after our ascent, I did not find this sense of relief. I felt really happy at the completion of the climb, but there was also another feeling concerning the progression in climbing that I have tried to explain. The Eiger was 6,000 feet high and three-quarters of a mile wide at the base. It seemed a lot of rock to have only one route. Ideas for a new route began to form.

It was not until I met John Harlin that I found someone who was interested in such a project. He was more than interested; he had already taken part in two attempts to establish a new line up the Face, once in winter 1964 and again in June of that year. The high point had been the Second Icefield. What they were trying in fact was an old start, with a direct finish from the Death Bivouac upwards. They did not use the start of the usual Heckmaier route but climbed directly up the rock buttress taken by the first pair to try the face, Sedlmayer and Mehringer in 1935. But ideas were

71

developing for a more ambitious project. I have already explained how the direttissima concept had gained great momentum in the Dolomites. Harlin had tried to apply it on attempts at the West Face of the Dru direct. So why not a direct route on the Eiger?

We quickly realized that a project such as this would have to be tackled in winter. Any direct route would come in direct line of Spider fire. Only in winter is the stonefall frozen.

In February 1965 John and I decided to make a close reconnaissance of the face. The main barrier to a direct route seemed to be a cliff barrier about 300 feet high which stretched at the level of Eigerwand Station all the way from the North-West Ridge to the Hinterstoisser Traverse. It had been climbed on its extreme right by Sedlmayer and Mehringer, but this was too far over for a direct route. We wanted to examine the possibilities in the region of Eigerwand Station.

Telescope study is never satisfactory, so we decided to go on to the wall proper. As it was only a recce, a little cheating seemed to be in order.

We could not go out of the window at Eigerwand Station without being discovered. To be in the tunnel at all was strictly forbidden unless in emergency, and punishable by a large fine. By careful study of old plans, John had found that there was an old refuse opening just short of Eigerwand Station. This seemed to be for us. Chris Patterson, a British climber working in Leysin, and Bob Boucher came along to help carry equipment. We caught the last train up to Eigergletscher Station, and tried to be as inconspicuous as four laden climbers can be in a ski resort. To baffle the station authorities, we ploughed off round a corner in the direction of the Mönch and sat out of sight waiting for darkness to fall. Soon we were tramping up the tunnel and after about two hours found the shaft we were looking for. This looked particularly good for staying unnoticed. There was an initial room with some tools in it, then another with a window opening out onto the Face. It was a weird experience the next day, slipping out of the window onto the wall. From our comfortable bivouac hole straight into the Eiger winter.

It was as I was to find it on many future wintry days. Shadowy, very cold, with a slight wind blowing spindrift in all directions. Up to our waists in powder, we ploughed leftwards towards Eigerwand

Station. A very impressive wall, this first band. A few lines of weakness, but none that could by any stretch be called easy. Pensively, we returned to our cave at nightfall. Having effected that part of our recce, the next day John and I climbed most of the Sedlmayer–Mehringer buttress for training. I led and found it hard. Certainly it was winter and covered in powder and this made it very difficult, but one could see that even in dry conditions it was a formidable piece of climbing. Abseiling back down, I felt a lot of respect for those two who had tackled the cliff on sight on their first visit to the Western Alps.

As we climbed through the window, a train drew up outside and loud knocks began at the door. We had made a barrier of wood but it seemed as if we were discovered anyway, so we let in the railway officials. We were prepared for the worst, police and fines, but for once the officials seemed friendly. Amused by our wanderings, they said we had been spotted on the first day but it had taken them two days to find our whereabouts. Their initial thinking was that we were on a full-scale attempt and had started from the bottom. But when extensive telescope inspection failed to reveal tracks, they had come to the conclusion that we were either supernatural or using the tunnel. They did not even put us on a train but allowed us to walk out. This was unheard of: penniless climbers in the past had often been forced onto the train and charged a first-class fare which they could ill afford.

One thing remained in our minds after this recce—a direct route would be a formidable problem. We planned to make an attempt the next winter.

During that summer John and I had a temporary altercation and split up. But as I was languishing back in Scotland he had been planning carefully, and had organized newspaper support for the climb which meant that a team could be equipped with the best equipment. After being turned down by various climbers, he eventually decided to patch up the quarrel and rang me up at Christmas. Not being proud where a new route on the Eiger was concerned, I quickly accepted. A further telegram brought me rushing straight from Ben Nevis to Leysin to find John and Layton Kor, one of America's best climbers. Old feelings were quickly lost in enthusiasm for the new project.

Our plan was to go onto the wall and hope to climb through in ten days. This was based on John's and my own previous knowledge of the Face, a helicopter reconnaissance in February just after my arrival in Leysin, and extensive study of photographs taken at that time. The only essential, but a very elusive one, was ten days of good weather.

There is a great weight problem in putting equipment and food for ten days on the backs of three people and still being able to climb upwards. Everything has to be selected with a view to weight. Ounces count. Even with the climbing equipment slung round our bodies the sacks would weigh around thirty pounds. This is too heavy for actual climbing and necessitates sack hauling. As for food, we could only budget minimally for ten days. Some dried meat, bacon, nuts, chocolate and a few hot drinks per man-day. In a period of ten days with extreme cold thrown in this means that your performance level is always decreasing slightly. One bad storm can put you close to the edge.

Knowing these problems we sat for three weeks in Kleine Scheidegg, monitoring weather forecasts twice a day. We really worked on the system. Phone-calls to Geneva, Zurich and London. There were occasional good days, but no sign of the settled period we wanted. Ten days is a lot of fine weather to ask for, but we had good precedents; in the previous two winters there had been even longer spells.

Towards the end of February, we decided to go back to Leysin for a couple of days, the weather still being unsettled. No sooner had we arrived than a panic-stricken phone-call came from Chris Bonington at Kleine Scheidegg saying that eight Germans had started up our route using fixed rope tactics. Shattered, we turned right round and shot back.

Chris and Peter Gillman were covering the story for the *Daily Telegraph*, Chris to come some way with us on the wall and Peter to write the basic story. Looking for pictures, Chris had followed the Germans to the foot of the wall. At that time they hadn't been too friendly, throwing snowballs as he approached with cameras at the ready. But he had seen enough to find out their plan of campaign. Their intention was to use expedition tactics; that is, fixing ropes and establishing camps with four lead climbers and four behind carrying supplies. Though not so pure as our concept this technique had the advantage that it could be used in bad weather. It was slow, but on

French Alps, Gran-des Jurrasses.

Left: Dougal Haston's nose has been cut by a piece of falling ice.

Main picture: Dougal Haston ice climbing on a new route on the North wall.

Eiger Direct
Expedition
1966.

Far right:
Dougal Haston
in a snow cave

Right: The
team at the
foot of Eiger

Main picture:
Dougal Haston,
left, John
Harlin, right.

Annapurna
South Face
Expedition
1970.

Far left: Dougal
Haston and
Mick Burke

Left: Dougal
Haston, Tom
Frost and Don
Williams

Everest
Expedition
1975

Main picture:
Dougal Haston
on the summit
of Everest.

Right:
Dougal Haston
on the lower
slopes of the
South West
face of Everest.

Main picture and right: Dougal Haston on an attempt on a minor peak above Rhamani glacier, near Changbang, 1974

most days progress could be made and if really bad weather came in retreat could always be made down the fixed ropes.

A dilemma for us. Do we still wait for good weather and try the single push? If good weather didn't come then the Germans would be pushing steadily up the wall while we waited at the bottom, an almost intolerable state of affairs for our climbing minds. Also, if a push attempt was turned back by bad weather then we'd really be far behind. The weather forecasts were still mediocre, so the only solution seemed to be to resort to expedition tactics as well. This we did. . . .

The conflict is fierce. Two separate parts of time and space are fighting their respective battles. I, a free being, am existing, but the fact of my existence has long ceased to give me trouble. It is where I am at present that is causing mental turmoil. The time late March 1966; the place, the Eiger Nordwand.

The second conflict is certain parts of Nature having private battles of their own. Though of late there seems to be some form of unison, in that everything seems to be determined to wipe this minute thinking object from the huge inanimate wall, where many think he has no right to be.

I am sitting with part of my right leg on the ice; the left one swings in a sling on the steep slope. A sodden, then frozen, sleeping-bag stirs memories of warmth from forgotten corners of the senses. The storm has been going on for two days; two of the many of striving to make this direct route exist. Our seeking to make a new line on this, the greatest north wall, has brought us to our present position.

The 'us' are myself and four Germans. Two, Roland Votteler and Sigi Hupfauer are ten feet to my right, crouching crampon-held under a red tent sack. The others, Jorg Lehne and Günter Strobel, are somewhere above, minute, sling-held spots in this morass of Nature's purgatory. I have just descended from above to find some sleeping gear. There would have been no survival without. We had been a bewildered three up above, lost in the storm, seeking the elusive Summit Icefield but unable to find it and wearied by the unrelenting difficulty. Sleep is not possible as my position is directly in an avalanche chute, and every so often I have to heave as much as I dare to disturb a huge mass of powder snow. Slowly I drift into a dream state and begin to reconsider the four weeks of effort that have led me to this position.

A February day and we were four at Scheidegg. John Harlin, Layton Kor and I, with Chris Bonington as photographer, a role which was to change. Thoughts of having hallucinations when eight figures appeared on 'our' direct line. But a confirmation by many pairs of eyes affirmed reality. They retreated that day, and we found out that they were eight Germans from Stuttgart: Jorg Lehne, Peter Haag, Günter Strobel, Sigi Hupfauer, Roland Votteler, Karl Golikow, Günter Schnaidt, Rolf Rosenzopf.

An interruption by an avalanche destroys my recall. Slowly I wriggle the snow into space and settle down once again to my dreaming. When sleep is not possible, dreaming is a great way of time-passing on bad bivouacs. Recalling worrying moments that have been overcome often makes the present bad seem better. All is not clear in my mind at the moment, only certain incidents keep flashing back.

The difficult ice climbing, where we had thought it would be easy, leading up to the first band. Two days of sitting in slings above Eigerwand Station window, admiring the superb piton artistry of Layton Kor as the rope went out and out through pitons that seldom went in over an inch; a web of blind cracks that would have had most people fumbling. The day we finished the band there was an abseil for me that almost ended in disaster. A 300-foot free drop and an upside-down flip in the middle as I tangled with the climbing rope. Fortunate extraction by a knife from below.

The days above, leading to the second band, are a blur of crampon-strained calves and aching axe-arms overcoming seventy-to-eighty-degree thin-ice-plated slabs. Climbing parallel with the Germans to the top of the second band, then on over varying types of ground with one thing in common, seldom easy, to the Second Icefield and up to the crest of the Flatiron in a storm. A glorious day, with Layton on the Third Icefield. Then six days in a snow hole on the Death Bivouac with John. These six days of confinement are still vivid in my mind. There were immense problems in just staying alive. The constant battle to keep spindrift off our down clothing; freezing hands fumbling with petrol stoves which would not light; long periods during the day when nothing would ease the aching cold in one's limbs; functional problems; psychological problems; trying not to quarrel over petty things; talking to pass the long hours on almost every conceivable subject; sleep which was often disturbed by insidious spindrift, when one had to emerge from deep stupor to brush it off, only to find half an hour later that the same thing had happened again: food running out on the fourth day and eventual defeat on the sixth, as we were forced to go down just as the weather turned reasonable again.

Then the struggle of Layton and Chris as they gradually solved the problems beneath the Spider and Layton's amalgamation with the Germans to reach the Spider as Chris came down.

John and I were by then fit and reascended to the Death Bivouac to be greeted by a fresh bad-weather forecast. Layton went down and no sooner had he disappeared than we heard by radio that the Germans were in the Fly and we set off for the summit. I had left the Death Bivouac with a cheerful 'see you in the Spider' to John. I never saw him again. A broken fixed rope ended the life of one who belonged to the finest of men. The whole climb had lain in the balance, but the thought of establishing the direct route as a memorial to John had overcome our urge to flee as we were rocking in the throes of bitter defeat. We five had been left to go for the summit. All below went down and stripped the face of fixed ropes.

The day after the accident the forecast storm had broken. It was savage, but we were determined. The achievement of the climb of our dreams was at hand and the storm gradually became the norm. After two days of fighting upward in it, clear days seemed to belong to memory. Günter and Jorg had pushed up the summit cliffs and then descended to a communal bivouac in the Fly under the impression that the major difficulties were over. Jorg and I had set out today to finish the climb and had ended up in our present position. The difficulties were still all too painfully obvious. My reflections put me in a euphoric state. This was slowly but systematically shattered as a greyish light began to assert itself over the black of the night. Dawn was here and all was not ended, so there had to be movement.

I unbend, creaking from the tent sack, and start to put on crampons. No need to describe the painfulness of this task. A thorough physical and mental check is then made. Both pass. I feel capable of days of struggle physically. My mind is now in a strange state of blank acceptance. It does not seem as if anything can get worse. The avalanches are pouring down the cracks. The nightmare wind whirls round in the bowl of the face, whipping snow in all directions. My eyelashes, nose and mouth are quickly plastered by a huge ice crust. I can hardly see Sigi and Roland ten feet to my left. The only link with those above is the ghostly line of the fixed rope that I had to come down the night before: an inanimate umbilical cord linking us to a mountain that seems only to want to reject those gathered on its flanks. I quickly move up this rope to try and catch Jorg and Günter. But there is no sign of them at the bivouac site, only a forty-foot gap in the fixed ropes. The immediate impulse is to try it alone, but I decide to wait on my two companions. There is a long period of reflection on the stance before they arrive. They look fantastic: completely white, with great long icicles hanging like fangs from nose and mouth. The gap is overcome and we three progress. A gap in the cloud suddenly reveals Jorg and Günter just disappearing out of sight. We are on the Summit Icefield. Jubilation, then worry. I can't see a continuance of the fixed rope. We are on blank sixty-degree water ice. I eventually see rope 150 feet above. We have no ice-axes, no hammers, only one ice-piton. I fill in the gap. It is the nearest I have gone to the limit.

I was in a position to look out over the edge of all things as I at last grasped the fixed line. An hour later it was done. The memorial to John exists. The Eiger has lost its toughest battle....

The descent down the West Flank was wonderful. I was met on the summit by Chris Bonington, who showed the way to a snow-hole about a thousand feet down. An amazing place—a four-man cave with twelve people crammed into it. As well as the German team and myself, there were Chris, Mick Burke and Toni Hiebeler. The whole trip nearly ended in suffocation due to the excess of Gauloise smoke. There was so much snow on the West Flank that it was one long glissade down to the tumult at Eigergletscher. Press, television, the whole place was in an uproar. My fingers were frostbitten. I only wanted to rest and talk quietly to friends. But it was not possible— Press conferences, telephone-calls, telegrams, and parties in the evening. Mick and I nearly got lost coming from the German Pension to Scheidegg Hotel in a blizzard; that would have been a great piece of news.

Three days later I was in hospital in London. My fingers looked bad. Mike Ward, the Everest doctor, recommended an experimental treatment—hyperbaric oxygen. I spent ten days in the London hospital, joined half-way through by Chris who had frostbitten feet. Thanks to the treatment and the incredible care of the staff, I walked out after the ten days with no fingernails, badly withered fingers, but no amputations. I'll never forget stepping outside. It had been a worrying period. Life could go on. What use is a fingerless mountaineer? Chris also came out unscathed. I wish I could say the same for my German friends. Of the four who climbed out with me, three, Lehne, Strobel and Votteler, went into hospital for frostbite. A few weeks later I received a letter from Jorg Lehne: '*I have had my right big toe amputated, Gunter and Roland have both lost all their toes but are bearing up very well.*' A shattering letter. But a climber can recover from lost toes, even though it is a long painful process. I wondered what could have happened if I hadn't come back to Britain. It had been a costly climb in human values—one life, twenty-one toes, and weeks in hospital.

Controversy raged for a long time after. The use of fixed ropes was condemned. Many climbers entered the issue with sweeping statements about the ethics of the route. The moment something new and controversial is done, some climbers seem only too willing to get up and shout about the wrongness of it all. What causes this? We had just established the hardest route in the Alps. Our tactics were new. But the environment was new. We had envisaged using classical methods, but at the time they proved impossible. But these people who had not dared were now coming out of their holes to criticize. Was it envy? Insecurity? I'll never know, but it left a sad impression on me that people could be so petty.

For most of the German team, the Eiger was the high point of their climbing careers. Layton Kor retired to become a Jehovah's Witness. For myself, I felt as if I had just come at last out of the darkness into the light, and the exploration of that light offered so many bewildering possibilities that my mind could scarcely cope with the contemplation of it all.

The only cloud was that another friend was gone. John Harlin was a complex person. Talented in certain fields, he wanted to be good at everything: a dreamer who sometimes believed his dreams were reality. He died while fulfilling his greatest ambition, a direct route on the Eiger. Could that not be the best time to die? My relationship with him was brief and stormy. On the mountain everything worked well. He was like a general in a mountaineering hierarchy, planning, directing, conceiving new ideas. I often fulfilled the straight practical part of leading, doing the most difficult parts. Disliked by many, John hated people who were less strong than he was. He was used to holding court and having people listen to his every opinion. I often quarrelled violently with him. Perhaps the basis of our relationship was mutual respect rather than close friendship, yet in our six days of surviving on the Death Bivouac we had become very close. Basically both withdrawn people, it seemed as if we'd both been holding back. With the shutters down we began to find out a lot which would have made for a different future relationship if he'd survived.

I began to wonder about partnerships in climbing. A mountaineering relationship, at least in the highest climbing levels, is a very strong thing. Everything is laid bare. You know your partner's strengths and weaknesses, most of his hopes and ideals. You are both working at levels often close to the limit. It's a big responsibility to have another's life in your hands, or to trust yours completely to someone. Life on a mountain is basically unemotional, you are too used to seeing the other person in strict control. That is perhaps why, in the emotional free-for-all of normal living, you act as, or in fact are, different persons.

CHAPTER SEVEN

Alpine Winters

Winter climbing in the Alps is still a relatively recent thing. It only really got going in the sixties. As usual there had been a few people ahead of the times: in the fifties Walter Bonatti had made winter ascents on the Tre Cime de Lavaredo and the Brenva Face of Mont Blanc. French climbers René Desmaison and Jean Couzy had completed an ascent and descent of the West Face of the Dru. There didn't seem to be much evidence of a great interest in this form of climbing, on the surface at least. Maybe equipment had a lot to do with it. Himalayan gear was very clumsy, and the lightweight, warm material needed to combat the violence of an Alpine winter storm had not been produced.

The winter ascent by Toni Hiebeler, Anderl Mannhardt, Walter Almberger and Toni Kunshofer of the Eigerwand in 1961 hit the climbing world like something from outer space. None of the great north faces had been seriously attempted in winter before. In a beautifully planned and carried out climb, they had jumped right in and plucked one of the hardest. Hiebeler had designed special double boots to combat the high risk of frostbite.

It was just like taking out a plug. Very quickly the Matterhorn North Face and the Walker Spur on the Grandes Jorasses were done.

Interest was high but there was room for everyone. Unlike the summer, when there were hundreds of people floating around, winter offered a dimension of the sport for the very few. Everything was that much harder; even normal routes became very difficult. Approaches were often long and usually necessitated knowledge of Alpine skiing. The margins for error were small. Frostbite was always just round the corner. A big storm was a very serious thing. There was no way a mediocre climber could bluff his way up a

81

hard route as had sometimes happened in the summer: ability and experience had to be there and even then one could be fully extended. With the summer Alps becoming more and more crowded there were suddenly exciting new dimensions for the people who cared. It was relative to being back to the early nineteenth century, when most of the Alpine summits were still virgin.

That's why Alpine winter climbing had taken a stronger hold on my system than the summer. Anyway, I had taken over John Harlin's climbing school, and it now seemed that most summers would have to be sacrificed. This did not seem to matter too much: overcrowding was becoming common in high season. Even for climbs like the Walker, one was beginning to have to wait in line. This I did not like. Mingling with shouting crowds was not my idea of alpinism. So I turned to winter. Once above the ski-lift level it was still possible to have the whole of a range to one's self on a certain day.

Mick Burke and I had decided to get together and climb during the winter of 1967. We'd been friendly for a few years but had never actually climbed together. Mick, from Wigan, is small, bespectacled, outspoken and gregarious. I'm the opposite, but from the climbs he'd done there didn't seem any obvious obstacle to our making a good team. At the beginning of the winter we had a drunken argument in Leysin and went outside to have a fight, then decided that wasn't a good start for a potential North Wall duo, and that climbing was more important than hurt pride. Thereafter things flowed smoothly and another good climbing partnership began to materialize.

The North Face of the Matterhorn was high on my list. I'd been rejected on two summer attempts so wanted to try it in winter. My experience on the Eiger Direct had been invaluable. I now had no qualms about winter bivouacs or climbing in storms. It would be good to get away from the expedition concept, however, and climb free and upwards with the normal amount of gear in our rucksacks. It was a good climbing winter; very little snow had fallen, to the frustration of the skiers. We got into shape doing rock climbs around Leysin. By the beginning of February there were no more excuses for lingering.

Mick wanted to do a training climb before the Matterhorn. A little bit of discussion, and the Gervasutti Couloir on Mont Blanc de Tacul at Chamonix seemed to come out top of the list. The main reasons were its ease of access and the fact that it was a straight ice climb that should not take more than two days. The weather was brilliant as we dumped our packs at the ticket office on the Midi Téléférique. We were taking the last one up and the attendant was suspicious. 'You're not allowed to sleep up there. I won't sell you a ticket.'

I could see Mick bristling. Controlling myself, I produced my best smile and French.

'We're going to bivouac outside. I don't think you can prevent us doing that.'

Inwardly boiling, I felt like dragging this stupid idiot out of his snug box and spreading him all over the floor. But my smile kept up the act, and he handed over the ticket. I also knew that for five francs a head into a workman's palm we would be sleeping comfortably in a warm room in the top station, with an electric fire to add to the discomforts of our bivouac.

A good night passed. Struggling out in the dark at five o'clock we came across the first obstacle. Normally there is a trail from the Midi station leading out onto the Vallée Blanche, used by skiers in the spring—the Vallée Blanche is one of the most famous ski-runs in Europe. But this was still high winter, and the only exit that had been cleared was a refuse window out onto the North Face of the Midi. Wind whipping, head-lights wavering, morale low, we cramponned out into the darkness and the 50° slope. Hard ice and violent front-pointing soon jerked us into motion. We crossed to the col and wandered down to the glacier on the south side. A beautiful dawn, as we strung our way through the crevasses to the foot of the couloir, the monolithic Capucin appearing incredibly smooth in the first light. A quick glance up the couloir: powder snow on ice, but blocking the top was an immense ice cliff. It did not look like a nice thing to have hovering over one's head for a full day. But then we remembered it was winter, and if it was going to stay inactive now was the time, so it was on with the rope and into the attack. For about two-thirds of the gully we made good progress. But within a hundred feet conditions changed: black water ice underneath about four feet of powder. Swimming, sliding and scraping steps. Protection was minimal as the ice underneath was thin. Our Salewa ice-screws had frozen at the core, making them useless. But no real problems; enjoyment was there. In winter one expects a little bit of hardship. Slowly we carved our way out, and towards sunset I pulled up from the last rubbishy step and sprawled into the little nook beneath the cornice.

That would be our bivouac site. The cornice would be no problem as there was a gap on the left-hand side. Mick crawled along and stuck his head over. Quickly he came scurrying back. 'It's a good job we're here. There's a hell of a wind blowing on the other side.'

That made the bivouac all the more comfortable. In the morning it was still fine and we easily descended the crevassed face of Mont Blance de Tacul.

Within six days we were sitting in the Hörnli Hut at the foot of the Matterhorn. Twice before in summer I'd been knocked back from the North Face. To even things up I wanted a winter ascent. It's also the safest time to climb this face. In summer the ordinary North West or Hörnli Ridge of this beautiful mountain has been reduced to a gross piece of commercialism. Guides drag up clumsy and incompetent clients who only want to say they've climbed the Matterhorn; they sure as hell don't enjoy it. Even to say they've climbed it is a lie—usually they're dragged up on a very tight rope, and I've even seen the 'sympathetic' guides kicking these unfortunates downhill. The North-West Ridge flanks the North Face, and this constant clumsiness sends showers of stones down on ropes who are trying the face. It is one of the most famous Alpine faces, first climbed in 1935 by the Schmid brothers. It had had its first winter ascent in 1962, by the Swiss Paul Etter and Hilte von Allmen. If successful, ours would be the fourth in winter.

MATTERHORN NORDWAND

The winter dawn comes slowly. A weak sun drags a centuries-weary head from the joys of the south into the white northern hemisphere. The valleys lurk; caves full of sleepy people reluctant to part with the stale artificial warmth of humanly created heat. The mountains, however, in this season seem to regain their primitive virginal pride. No more do the howling, littering summer masses tramp their more accessible flanks. There are still the skiers but they only scratch the lower limbs.

The Matterhorn, mightier than most, thrusts up out of the dark valley of Zermatt. During this time all its flanks are difficult, but the most difficult of all is the sprawling mass to the north. The old adventurers always thought of the north as where the grim struggles and challenges were to be found. It is no different in modern climbing.

'Nothing left,' they say.

'No more great challenges,' cry the armchair critics.

'Modern youth has no courage,' comes the voice from the bars.

Come north in winter, old men.

Somewhere on the North Face, problems were whirling through the head of the taller of two figures, sitting slumped and apparently lifeless on a small, sloping ledge. There was a great struggle going on. He was being chased down a cul-de-sac by a huge, screaming crowd of armchair critics until he reached the end. They began to get violent. He felt himself going. Then suddenly woke up, having slipped off the ledge into the hammock which was supporting his feet.

'Christ, Mick, the sun's up'—my first words as I quickly adjusted to reality from the dream state. Mick seemed to have had better dreams, as it took minutes for him to adjust. We didn't talk much but started performing the small tasks of making some tea-water and gradually working some of the cold out of limbs. The dream-thoughts were gone. It had been a harder bivouac than most, even though the weather was fine. Just as we had been settling down, the tent sack had been seized by a traitorous gust of wind and had left us suddenly cold and staring at each other and wondering if the warmth of seconds ago had really existed. The wind had been strong, wintry cold, and had rattled all night in our frost-burned, staring-eyed faces. Cooking had been difficult. Only tepid drinks, which did not stir the ice in our bodies. It had been a night ripe for bitter dreams, but it is better to have bad dreams than good on a bivouac; waking up to harsh reality is less disappointing.

Until the vanishing tent sack the two previous days had been almost ideal. The general situation gave most of what we were seeking in climbing. Though totally different as persons, we came very close in our ways of thinking in situations like this. The weather had been cold and good, the climbing difficult. The Matterhorn looks at close range as if a heavenly action painter had hurled random rocks into the ice that had stuck there in the intense winter cold. A typical pitch is picking from one stone to another for 150 feet with not much chance of protection. It had been the essence of roped movement. One was utterly reliant on the man ahead: one slip and two were down. We had alternated leads and shared this heavy yet enjoyable responsibility, and the great feeling of being alone. If anything goes wrong it will be a fight to the end. If your training is good enough survival is there; if not nature claims its forfeit. This is the difference between winter and summer climbing. In summer if anything goes amiss there is a professional rescue service which can get you out of most places. The summits are accessible; there are wire cables, helicopters. But not in a winter storm. Helicopters are grounded. Normal routes can be incredibly difficult and beyond the skills of the average. It is left to the party to get itself out. This is one of the reasons for going at this time—it puts all the training, all the dreams to the real test. Do you really have a right to be there? If not, you will soon be found out. This is the spirit of climbing, reaching deep into the mind and extending the body to the full. This is one of the few ways that one can really find out what is inside the skin.

The blowing-away of the tent sack had put the red light of emergency on our ascent. We did not have to tell each other that another bivouac would be weakening. If the weather broke it would really be rough. We prepared to go that little bit faster. The summit had to be reached that day, and then there was the long way down to the Solvay bivouac hut on the Hörnli Ridge. A long day. Were we capable? The first pitch after a cold bivouac is always a test. Mick had led the previous day's, I had this one. Unwarmed muscles and mind grapple with the difficulties. One just has to move slowly. The hands go numb. You warm them up. You move on. It is like trying to solve a difficult anagram. Your moves seem jumbled and not in sequence. But it comes slowly, and you emerge from the blundering dark into the full force of free movement. So it continued. We reached the summit. For once the sum of the parts made a tremendous whole. It was all there, vivid and full, as we sat on the windswept peak. We had been masters of the mountain and ourselves for three brief days. The neighbouring ranges seemed to be in sympathy, silent, with perhaps a few faltering self-seekers on their flanks. But so few. The descent was the beginning of the decline into uncertainty. The experience had been known. It was stored in mind. But it was past.

ARGENTIÈRE

This little saga got into motion when Chris Bonington arrived in a
muddle of climbing and camera equipment in Leysin towards the
middle of March. Now Chris is wise enough seldom to go anywhere
unless he is paid for it. On this occasion, labouring under a heavy fee
and a commission to write about the Last Great Problems, he'd
decided to come out and photograph one of them: the North Face
Direct of the Droites at Chamonix. But these onerous professional
duties never diminished his enthusiasm for climbing. Action pictures
are always more exciting, so we decided to make an attempt on the
Face.

The Direct Route had first been climbed in 1955 by two French
climbers, Cornaux and Davaille. Up until 1969 it had been done
three times, and called the hardest mixed route in the Alps. A
winter ascent was at the top of many Alpine lists. The only serious
try in winter had been the previous year by my Eiger Direct friends,
Lehne, Strobel and Golikow. In bad weather, and using expedition
tactics, they had been sent scurrying back to Stuttgart when an
avalanche wiped out their camp beneath the face.

Chris and I wanted to break away from using fixed ropes. We
just carried enough ice-pegs to enable a retreat to be made down the
icefield.

The approach to the Argentière hut is on skis from the Grand
Motets téléférique. Packs were huge, but after a night in the Vagabond bar two skiing friends had been convinced of the beauty of
high mountain skiing and the necessity of carrying heavy packs to
strengthen their legs. Our packs, even with this help, were heavy.
I'd been carrying a 35-millimetre camera on a ski film all winter, so
didn't have any problems, but Chris had a little more trouble. His
skiing is roughly at the snowplough level, not good enough for the
crusty powder on the descent to the hut. The hut was empty—no
competition for one day at least. We settled down to cooking and the
start for the trip, where living in the hut was just about as exciting as
actual climbing.

Lying dozing in my sleeping bag, I'd just checked my watch:
2 a.m. It was cold, very silent. I buried deeper into the down. I was
in the light dream state that is usually the prelude to a big route.

Scared of oversleeping, I was snapped violently awake by noises from the floor above. Wide awake but extremely puzzled. There was no one in the hut and anyone arriving late at night would have had to step on our heads to get upstairs. The footsteps continued, louder, stamping down the stairs. A rattling on the latch as the door to our room was tried. I held my breath. It didn't open. The steps clomped back upstairs—silence. Perhaps it was all a dream.

Yet I was pretty certain. I also didn't feel like going to investigate. The supernatural was an unknown field to me, and also something I'd always been slightly afraid of. Within a few minutes it seemed as if nothing had happened.

Morning. The weather was bad. Cloud down to the hut and snowing lightly. Tea brewing, nothing to do but wait. Chris went outside, came back in and stood beside me shifting from one foot to the other. Looked as if he wanted to say something—he's not usually so diffident, normally he's in head first with his statements. At last he broke the silence.

'Ah . . . Dougal?'

'Yes, Chris?'

'Did you hear anything last night?'

It was out. I hadn't been dreaming: he had heard exactly the same things. For the same reasons he'd remained in his bag. Feeling brave, we combed the hut. Nothing. Looked around the veranda for tracks—still nothing. Tales of haunted huts were by no means unusual in climbing, but neither of us had experienced anything before.

The weather stayed mediocre. A recce was made to the foot of the face, but cloud stuck around and we couldn't see much. We still had another night to spend in the hut. I dozed till about midnight, then lay awake. Sure enough, there it was again. The same process. Descent of stairs, rattle of the latch, re-ascent, silence. I knew Chris was awake because he wasn't breathing. In whispers we checked it out, flashed a torch, looked into the corridor—nothing. But somehow neither of us felt like going upstairs. Known things were fine: our courage had been tested to the full on many occasions. But there is something about the unknown; you suddenly realize there are possible parts of the universe you know nothing about. Nothing could induce either of us to go upstairs. Back to bed still wide awake.

Still doubtful weather. The prevalent feeling was that the next night should be spent in the clean, cold air of a bivouac. It was still too risky to embark on something like the Droites, so we switched our thoughts to a lesser but still good objective; the North Face of the Argentière by the Lararde–Secogne route still awaited a winter ascent. It was accessible, though a long walk from the hut. We decided to go and bivouac at the foot that night. It was also the third last day of the recognized winter season, so we'd have to move anyway to get in an official winter ascent.

This arbitrary ruling that winter ends on 21 March seems somewhat ludicrous. On the Eiger Direct we finished on 26 March, and I still don't know if we are credited with just a first ascent or first and winter ascent—despite the worst storm of my life. Some friends of mine had made an ascent of the Gervasutti Pillar of Mont Blanc de Tacul from 22 to 25 March in a violent winter storm, and had been credited with the first spring ascent! How stupid! Winter should be flexible, but at least mid-December to mid-April.

The approach to the Argentière involves going over the Col du Chardonnet. With the fresh snow it looked like something of a long trudge.

Just before leaving the hut I found the climbs book, where everyone writes down their projected routes. Flicking through, I came to an interesting note for September: *Guardian killed by avalanche in the couloir on the Aiguille d'Argentière.* Sudden whirling thoughts: the guardian in summer usually got up around 2 a.m. to waken prospective climbers. Was his ghost still doing the rounds?

Five hours and much trail-breaking later, we were just short of the Col du Chardonnet. Looking down, I saw a column stringing up the Glacier, two in front then three. A glance at Chris. I knew what he was thinking. 'Do you think it's a party for the Droites?' We'd been feeling slightly guilty about avoiding the main issue as the weather was now fine. Indecision. Five hours is a lot to waste. They could have been skiers.

Our sense of competition overcame rational thoughts. Not being able to bear the thought of another party starting up when we had gone to something smaller, we turned and shot back towards the hut. On the glacier we met the party of three. Ski-pants, ski-boots—no rucksacks—heading back for Argentière village—first guess wrong. In the hut door to feel utter fools—the others were two skiers for the High Route. The weather was turning again. Reason at last prevailed. We'd have to leave early in the morning and try and climb as much of the Argentière as possible during the day. It would mean, however, another night in the hut!

But the crowds must have frightened off the guardian. That night there were no footsteps, and by 5 a.m. we were off into the night. Even with the tracks it took us four hours to reach the col. From there it was straight onto the face, powder snow on hard ice. Immediately I felt glad we hadn't gone to the Droites; it would have meant much step-cutting and a slow time. Here we didn't have to cut steps but the climbing was not too fast either. Kicking, packing and thrusting into the powder trying to consolidate weight-bearing steps. Once again our tubular screws froze up. By chance I'd brought some ordinary ice-pitons, so at least we could get some belay protection.

At nightfall we were over two-thirds of the way up. It had been a long day, and we decided to bivouac just as the sun set. Considering our combined experience this was a crazy decision. First, we sat down in a kind of trough. Secondly, we could have climbed the remaining four or five rope-lengths by head-torch. Thirdly, we had a prototype untried tent sack. Sitting on the step we decided to pull the sack over our feet and keep our heads out to enjoy the beautiful evening. Out with the stove; everything's calm; we start brewing tea. A little wind gets up. *Whoomp!* We're both coughing, spluttering and half buried. A spindrift avalanche had come right down the chute, filling up the tent sack and covering everything.

O.K. Stay cool. This wasn't the first time we'd been buried in spindrift. Empty out the tent sack. Turn it round. Put it over our heads. Great. We should have been in a warm cocoon, but the new-model sack only reached our knees. The wind strengthened, spindrift kept pouring down. Our heads were covered. That was fine, but the wind caught the powder and whipped it up into the sack. After hours Chris got some water melted. He moved to tell me; over it went. So much was going wrong that I burst out laughing. There was no point in being angry any more. Sometime in the night tea was created, and everything seemed better. But it was a good job we could climb out in the morning. Our sleeping-bags were frozen, and would become sodden when packed in rucksacks. It would have been certain retreat on the Droites—perhaps the ghostly guardian had been trying to warn us. Gladly we got going at first light and soon we were on the ridge in the sun, forgetting all about our frozen twelve hours. How quickly the trained mind adapts! Back to the hut by midday: only unusual things were Chris falling half-way into a crevasse and finding a mammoth avalanche across our original tracks.

The incidents didn't let up until we reached Chamonix. Our exit rucksacks were gigantic. I was carrying about seventy pounds, Chris about sixty, but with the state of his skiing that was equivalent to about a hundred and ten. On the long traverse to the Longan station, I caught an edge and went about a hundred feet down a steep slope. My heavy sack kept rolling me over and over. The bindings didn't come loose. Certain broken leg, I thought. However, it seemed to be a trip of many but not serious incidents, and there were no breaks. Chris was falling every second turn, pack pile-driving his head into the snow. Somehow we got down. We blew expenses on a luxury hotel and collapsed dreaming of spindrift and the supernatural.

CHAPTER EIGHT

Old Man of Hoy

Sitting in Leysin after the Matterhorn, in the pleasant contemplative relaxation that follows a successful major climb, I really began to feel strongly about living in the Alps. True, I'd spent seven months of the previous year in those very regions. But it always had had the feeling of a transitory state; Scotland was still vaguely home. I'd been involved in so many happenings that I hadn't sat down and contemplated for a long time. Now everything became clear all of a sudden. Scotland didn't mean much to me any more. Before I am eternally damned, let me say that I mean this on a climbing level. I had done as much as I had wanted to in that country. To stay there would have been to stagnate. I was committed to climbing, I had to go on to larger projects. At the end of the previous summer, I'd been asked to take over John Harlin's climbing school. This was another good reason for staying: an interesting project, it had run for only a year when he was killed. Now I was really interested in taking the roots of a good idea and applying my outlook on climbing to the running of the establishment. I knew it would be the struggle that all projects are in infancy. But it was something exciting within climbing, which wasn't for once in the range of direct challenge to mountain ways. I'd been climbing for so long in the insular world of the extreme that I hadn't really thought too much about passing on my skills to others. Did I really want to? On reflection the answer seemed to be yes, provided the people concerned were enthusiastic and keen to learn. I'd had so much enjoyment out of the mountains and had been the recipient of so many valuable lessons in my youth, that it would have been very narrow-minded to deny the benefit of my experience to anyone who was genuinely interested.

The attractions of Leysin were many. Situated in the Vaudoise Alps above Lake Geneva, it was only two hours' drive from Chamonix,

Grindelwald or Zermatt—just like going from Edinburgh to Glencoe. The local limestone was also very good. The common impression of going to live in a mountain village is that one has suddenly turned into a hermit and wants to shut off from civilization. The contrary reigns in Leysin. A ski resort, it is the home of Club Vagabond. The school was started in 1961 by Allan Rankin, Carol Rankin, Luc van der Kaay and Joan Seeman. Since then it has become a meeting-place for travellers from all over the world. There is a constant influx of new people, alive people, many of them interesting to talk to. Horizons broaden instead of stagnating. I made up my mind to stay.

Spring was beautiful that year. By April the crocuses and daffodils were thrusting through the fast fading winter snows. Dave Agnew was in Leysin, and we did a lot of training together: two idyllic weeks in the sun- and sea-soaked Calanques outside Marseilles; new routes on the local cliffs; long walks in the pre-Alps; lazy nights in the Vagabond. The school was opening in June. I came back from a weekend in Paris to a letter from the B.B.C.:

> We are planning another climbing television programme. This time the subject is the Old Man of Hoy, and we are planning to transmit the programme live on Saturday and Sunday, 8 and 9 July. We shall have three ropes of two climbers each, and so far I have had acceptances from Joe Brown, Chris Bonington, Pete Crew, Tom Patey and Ian McNaught Davis. I wonder whether you would also like to take part and lead one of the ropes.

I knew that the Old Man was a 400-foot sandstone sea-stack off the coast of the island of Hoy in the Orkneys. It had been climbed for the first time in the summer of 1966 by Chris Bonington, Tom Patey and Rusty Ballie. They took the easiest-looking line, but even that was graded Very Severe. Photographs looked very impressive. There was a chance of new routes.

O.K., why not? My first course was due to start, but I left Davie in charge and hopped on the plane. I caught a glimpse of the Old Man as we were coming in to land: it had an impressive air about it. Though only 400 feet high it looked much larger because it was set apart.

We crossed to the island of Hoy by small boat and found a hive of activity at the other end. The Army had set up camp and were helping with the carrying of supplies and cooking. Peter Crew was to be my climbing partner, and instead of following Joe Brown and McNaught Davis up the South Wall as originally intended we now had the choice of trying the South-East Arête, which lay between the original route and the South Face. I was much happier about this: as far as lines go, it looked the best on the pinnacle. After an easy first pitch there was a series of overlapping roofs leading to a big ledge, followed by a line of cracks and chimneys to the top.

The idea of following another party had lacked a lot of potential excitement—it would have been one of those dangerous 'lesser climbs' with their consequent slacking of concentration. There was no doubt about the difficulty of the new route. Work would have to start straight away if we were to be able to get up it on the day of transmission. The idea was to prepare the roofs up to the ledge, fixing the pitons so that we could make a smooth ascent on the Saturday evening when the first transmission was to go out. Not theoretically live, but it would have made much less good viewing if people had had to watch me tackling and pinplacing on the roof.

Sandstone is probably one of the toughest tests of artificial technique. The cracks on the arête are short and blind, with a brittle edge. None of the pitons would go in all the way. In this event you have to tie short slings round the part closest to the rock to reduce leverage—if a carabiner is put directly through the eye of a short-driven piton and pulled on, in all probability it will come out. If you clip the carabiner into the sling and then pull, it usually stays in place.

Though only 150 feet above the sea, the route felt just as exposed as the Cima Ovest in the Dolomites. I led this part. Initially it went slowly, as I was desperately trying to avoid placing bolts. By devious methods the first roof succumbed in traditional style, but the wall above was a real horror-show. The only cracks were about two to three inches wide and a half-inch deep. At first I got away with bongs, the largest angle pitons put in lengthways in six-inch cracks and tied off. But this was too dangerous for continuous use, as a fall would probably have stripped the whole pitch. So a bolt had to be placed. Eventually I had to place a few more to reach the stance. The plan was to climb this pitch on Saturday and bivouac on the ledge; that would leave the whole of Sunday to complete the rest of the route.

The day arrived. It was a strange feeling to be standing on the ledge ready to start performing. There was a radio mike around my neck and headphones inside my helmet. I thought of the many years of solitude on isolated faces; now there were a few million people watching and Chris Brasher's commentary straight in my ears to disturb the concentration.

I often wonder why climbing has become so popular as a television spectacular. The movements are fairly slow and repetitive. Visually, I don't think it's too exciting. Are they waiting for someone to fall off?

It was a cold night, with a strong wind whipping spume off the sea. The go signal came through. Immediately I forgot about the outside factors and became engrossed in climbing the pitch. Brasher kept switching from party to party, asking questions. But my radio mike was playing up so none of my comments came through. I could also hear the other parties acting their parts: Brown in his flat drawl explaining every move, McNaught Davis grunting and heaving, Bonington giving a seminar on climbing technique and Patey being plain humorous, pirouetting on his jumars.

The bivouac was one of my toughest. We lay on the ledge in sleeping-bags and foam mattresses and hauled up a hot meal and a bottle of whisky from the girls on the ground below. One could even read by the powerful lamps on the mainland—the Old Man was floodlit.

The Sunday weather was again reasonable. Dull and windy but at least not raining. Our route continued in fine style, with a series of short cracks, overhanging walls and chimneys. Brasher's eagle eye always seemed to spot when you were on a difficult part, so the viewers would often get gasping, unrehearsed answers to his questions. We were the last to finish and found the whole group sitting drinking tea on the summit.

It had been planned that Bonington should do a 450-foot abseil straight down to give a last little titbit to the viewers. Now Christian was having second thoughts about the friction created by his descendeur. It would have been an unhappy ending, though perhaps a commercially good one, if the rope had melted on the way down sending Chris to a hero's end in the waves. Good television performer as he is, there was a limit to what Chris would do for the public, so he compromised by being lowered on a pulley from the top. The rest of us slid down the normal route in more traditional fashion. After an impressive party supplied by the happy B.B.C., I was soon on my way back to Leysin, a summer of instruction, and dreams of Cerro Torre.

CHAPTER NINE

Cerro Torre

After the Eiger it seemed as if the time had come for a visit to some range farther away than the European Alps. As far back as 1962 I had contemplated going to the Baltoro Spires in the Karakoram range in Pakistan, but this had fallen through because of permission problems. Since then I had been so involved in Alpine events that I'd scarcely thought too much about going elsewhere. Nepal was closed to expeditions during this period, and when an area has been closed for a time it often begins to seem in one's mind that it will never be reopened. Consequently I'd stopped dreaming about big peaks.

I was living in London for a couple of months prior to the winter, when Mick Burke rang me up.

'What do you think about going to Cerro Torre? A four man expedition with Martin Boysen and Pete Crew.' Martin Boysen, a Manchester schoolteacher, I knew well, but I hadn't climbed with on a big route. Tall, lean and very relaxed, he gives an impression of laziness until he starts to climb. He had the reputation of being one of the best rock-climbers in Britain. That didn't mean to say he hadn't climbed any ice. He'd done some of the best Scottish routes, and all this combined with a formidable Alpine record made me feel good about having his company.

Pete Crew, a twenty-five-year-old computer programmer, also had a strong reputation as a rock climber, and I'd enjoyed climbing with him on the Old Man of Hoy. So all in all the team sounded strong. It would need to be!

The mountain sounded not so familiar. I knew that it was in Patagonia; also that it was reputed to be very hard. From reading Bonatti's book I remembered that he hadn't climbed it. That in itself meant something. Anyway, I said yes, provisionally, I would come to a meeting in a week's time, and set about doing some research. Here's what I came up with:

> The combination of high technical difficulty and an extremely exposed location make the Cerro Torre one of the most formidable and dangerous problems known to man. The mountain is situated on the edge of the continental ice-cap and is the most westerly of the Fitzroy group. Because of this, Cerro Torre and its satellites take the full brunt of the winds and mists that sweep across the cap. The mountain becomes plastered with snow and ice during bad weather, and on the few occasions when the sun penetrates the mist the ice melts rapidly and avalanches down the 5,000-foot rock walls. Even during sunny spells the wind seldom drops. Exposed ridges are impossible to climb under these conditions. Fitzroy, only two miles away to the east, has an ice-free west face and rather better weather as it is always in the Torre's rain shadow.

Interesting!

The actual history was more tantalizing. We knew about Bonatti's attempt, but Cesare Maestri, an Italian, had claimed an ascent in 1959 with Austrian Toni Egger. However, an avalanche on the descent had killed Egger, and there were no photographs. Maestri had been rescued delirious at the bottom. In his later account everything was vague: no positive technical reports. A lot of doubt remained. His story could be neither proved or disproved.

After seeing photographs and reading these facts there was no stopping. We had to go. The Maestri–Egger route had been the South-West Ridge. We proposed to attempt the untried South-East Ridge. It looked easier.

Planning went ahead for the next nine months. There were two additions to the party, José Fonrouge, the best Argentinian climber, and Peter Gillman to cover the story for the *Sunday Times*.

The gear left in mid-November by ship for Buenos Aires, Mick and I with it. Three weeks of hedonism before the struggle ahead. It is a good thing to have contrasts like this. One cannot live at the extreme all the time; the tenseness and strain would drive one over the edge. A few weeks of good food, easy living and female company are good training for coming ordeals. One gets tired of the easy life but is relaxed in mind, and the contrast makes the eventual hardship seem more appealing.

From now on I will give straight passages from what I wrote during the long spells of inactivity on the trip, setting down the vivid impressions of a first expedition.

Arrival in B.A. is amusing. One gets used to a ship, and suddenly we are all alone in a foreign land, so to speak. But Fonrouge was waiting for us, and during the first day all the gear was transported through Customs and stored until the time for our flight south. (This in South America was equivalent to a miracle. It had once taken Whillans six weeks to get his gear cleared.) The time until departure was spent pleasantly meandering around, with a few parties in the evening. B.A. is a pleasant city; reminds me a lot of Paris. It is spring, with cafés spilling onto the pavements and trees in blossom everywhere. Sunday morning early we were driven out to an army airport. Then followed eight hours and 1,500 miles in a due-for-pension DC3 to Comodoro Rivadavia, an ugly oil town on the south-east coast. What is puzzling to someone who has not been outside Europe before is the astonishing vastness. Often it is not waste, but mile upon mile upon hundreds of miles of grass, lakes, cows, sheep and very few humans. Comodoro was reached on Sunday night. The majority of our equipment was supposed to be coming down by truck on Monday morning from B.A. We slept out on a windy sleepless night. It was three days before the gear arrived, and many hours until we sweated the last box onto a well laden truck. This was followed by an all-night drive south-west. Nothing but dusty roads and headlights, changing to morning sun and a drop in temperature as 500 miles farther south we appear. Then mile after mile towards our mountain, to be fetched up short in the late afternoon by a river which couldn't be crossed by truck. Eventually we came to an arrangement whereby the Argentinian army camped at the other side promised to take our gear to the road end. From there it would be by horses to base camp.

Our immediate problem was the hundred-yard carry across the shaky bridge with a ton of gear. Problem solved by three hours of bruised shoulders and strain. The Torre was still hiding. Brief glimpses of Fitzroy had come through, showing much snow low down. It was very reminiscent of the Alps in late spring. The army arrived in the early evening, happy and helpful with the gear loaded quickly and contentedly leaving the wind- and sand-blown camp. The new camp was in a field beside a remote Customs post on the Chile border, and supposedly three hours from base camp. Problems at the moment were ways of transportation. The alternatives were horses or, more doubtful, a gendarmerie helicopter. The helicopter of course would be much better, as it would be done in a few hours as opposed to a few days. But as the Torre had not appeared out of the cloud, time was not as yet a particular problem.

Gone were the expectations of sitting in shorts and sunbathing at base camp. Even this relatively well sheltered spot was cold, like camping in Scotland in the autumn. The state of mind necessary was obviously that of previous waits for big climbs. A deep relaxation, and time spent in reading and writing, with reluctant excursions outside for the menial but necessary tasks like cooking and organizing gear.

Yesterday (1 December) passed mainly in this fashion. Firewood is plentiful so we can cook over open fires. Ate supper with the gendarme and family. Today similar. Two days merge into one very easily. The important thing here is not to lose patience. We are at present awaiting horses and always horses will come tomorrow. It's now Monday and the horses are supposed to come on Tuesday, but they were also supposed to come on Saturday and Sunday—who knows? For the first time we are running into the famous 'mañana' of Spanish countries.

Went walking yesterday in the general direction of base camp. Dead country, flat, with shrivelled witch-forest trees and dull glacier-filthied streams, but for once with the Torre in the background. A problem it certainly should be, with, from this distance, still no obvious cracks in the defensive system of the final tower.

The transition to torpor during the waiting days is not too difficult. Obviously. There will soon be lots of action, and the very fact of being here, to be able to lie under the sky dreaming, is a glorious transition. There is a working radio. We hear the news in English but it all seems so unconnected. The temptations and jealousies of the social world are not here, and while one would not wish it as a permanent way of life it is a necessary part, just as going to cities occasionally is a necessary part. The two contrasting parts make for a reasonably well adjusted whole. One does not stagnate in this manner.

The horses arrived and three days of transportation began. On the second day, I shouldered a load and left the valleys for base. Found a leafy glade in the woods with the weather fine and the Torre dominating the upper reaches of the glacier. The next day I was left alone in base so made the effort of packing a load of rope and set off in the general direction of the Torre.

The weather is mediocre. Very little of the peaks is showing. The rucksack is ungainly and heavy, walking is bad. I soon lose any semblance of trail and end up leadenly plodding over steep moraine. Higher up the infamous Patagonian wind is blowing, with heavy black puffball clouds spitting horizontal rain onto the naked body. This is the dull necessity of forcing a route. The gear has to go up. Good days should be for climbing, therefore bad days for the porter work. It seems logical, but often accepting logic is not easy. Lonely and dull-thinking I plod on and dump my load beneath the water-spewing cracks. The next day is the violent contrast that you are told to expect on this area: sun, blue sky and shining summits. I go back up with Fonrouge. More loads. The walk is still tedious but the scenery compensates.

Rounding the corner of the glacier and into what is almost an ideal mountain panorama. Fitzroy, Poincenot and satellites rockily bounding the right, rounding off towards Pere Giorgio at the head of the valley and swinging down in a difficult-to-comprehend glance at the staggering Torre. Where else is there such a mountain? The eye searches vainly for weakness in the final tower. Only close inspection will tell. But what a long way for possible disappointment! There can be no pointing with finger on photograph with this one; we must climb and explore. Even with perfect weather success is not certain. Leading down from the Torre and coming closely into the perspective of the fascinated watchers the view is completed by the icy wilderness of the east face of the Adella, 5,000 ft. of constant avalanche. We dump our loads and turn. Base finds Boysen. Crew is below with bronchitis.

Next day we all set out, intending to stay up and push on. Minus Fonrouge, we reached the high point in worsening weather, spent a wet night under a rock, returned. The wet night carried on into two sodden days which were spent sitting around base camp.

Eventually there was a clearance on the 13th. Mick went down to the lower camp to collect a tent while Martin and I hauled another set of loads up to the advance camp. Once again the afternoon rain set in, so we turned around and came straight back. The round trip was now taking us only five hours, a good sign of approaching fitness. In the evening Peter Crew turned up. He had flown out with Gillman and Boysen, and looked pale beside our marine sun-tan.

Thursday, 14 December: At present we are lying around waiting for the tent to arrive from base, with the hope that we can go up and establish a camp at the foot of the mountain, but it seems unlikely that there'll be much movement because of the high winds and the Torre still has its normal cloud cap showing. There is a vague type of weather pattern shaping. If it is a fineish morning, bad weather often creeps in during the late afternoon.

Friday. Our most productive day. Martin, Mick and I were off by seven o'clock. The weather looked overcast, but the wind had dropped and it now seems as if one must go, go, go, in any weather which however mediocre is that much better than pure bad. Moving much faster up the glacier, with the Torre thrusting through on occasion, we felt much fitter and advance dump came in two hours. A quick tea stop, some ropes and pegs in the rucksack, and we moved up towards the Torre. By this time the cloud had settled to its usual level and bad weather was again imminent, but this day we wanted to push at least as high as the start of the climbing. This we did, in warm sultry cloud with desultory snowflakes whirling around. The going was painful, knee-deep snow on crevasses and schrunded glacier with a good gain in height as well. The most we could see was up to the col, and accessibility looked reasonable as we studied. It looks to be about 800 feet, with an easyish rock start and a difficult ice-slab finish—we shall see. Down again, and, finding a valuable ice-cave at the edge of the glacier, we dumped the equipment and in the now total break moved back to base. A twelve-hour day, but productive. The next few days were spent supply hauling in poor weather. On Monday, the 18th, there was a total break and everyone stopped in base.

The weather in general seems to vary between bad and atrocious. A 'semi-reasonable' day is one which is cloudy with no break until 3 p.m. 'Bad' means raining all day. 'Atrocious' is a wet day with high winds. A 'good' day is going to mean an all-out push with no stops pulled—we might only get one a month. Wetness is a great problem. In bivouacs so far we have had to sleep in tent sacks because of drips. Condensation has made the bags wet by morning. It seems as if this will happen in all our bivouacs—a pleasant thought!

Right through over Christmas the weather was bad and miserable, but everyone adapted in his own peculiar way to time passing without too much frustration becoming apparent. Eventually there was a bettering on 27 December, and four British climbers went up to the ice-cave. The start of the way up to the col is a rock buttress with a ridge on top, which leads across a glacier to a face, which in turn leads to the ridge proper. Martin and Mick climbed the initial rock buttress. I prussiked up with a load and into a snow flurry, whence everyone scurried down to the cave.

Friday dawned hot, but we didn't start until late due to the great effort of moving. The tent is a haven relative to outside but still very damp, and one is loth to leave one's sleeping-bag to contemplate cooking. There was no wind, and the burning sun made the snow soft and the going hard for Martin and me as we ploughed up to yesterday's high point to start the slabby face to the col. Nasty snow with odd pitches of steep, rotten ice took us two-thirds of the way before we quit for the day. On the next we moved earlier but still latish, and some more of the same climbing saw Martin and me at the col. An impressive place: virgin, narrow and wind-punched. The view awesome: freak granite formations on the Torre; walls with cracks like scars—non-continuous; the avalanche-swept Maestri route. On the left, the Eigerish east face of the Adelle. Looking more and more a formidable problem. Straight down the sweep over Laguna Torre, past base camp to greenery and on to Lago Viedma. Very little sign of civilization. Out of rope, we descend again to the cave.

Sunday: Mick and Fonrouge up with loads to the col but couldn't advance because of the wind.

Monday: New Year's Day, Martin and I, 200 feet up the rocks above, then right down to rest. Weather seems to be holding. The climb is taking shape.

Tuesday: A wasted day due to laziness. Crew and Fonrouge responsible. Mick up to the ice-cave.

Wednesday: Fonrouge and Crew continue from our high point and make good progress up the crack systems to the top of the first step, Fonrouge leading all the way. On descending they found Mick at the col installed in a snow-cave that he had dug out. I went up to the lower cave and spent the night.

Thursday: Mick and Crew carry on the ridge work and once again make reasonable progress, Mick leading. One hard pitch up a nose in the buttress. They ended the day with a dilemma. Continuation up the ridge means climbing an overhanging nose; the alternative is to traverse right on very steep slabs into a dirty crack-cum-gully. I met them at the col after a heavy plough up in the mid-day sun. The bergschrund had collapsed and I spent some time trying to cross it, unsuccessfully, falling into the hole twice before traversing and climbing an ice pitch at the side. Found Fonrouge lying in the cave and tried to dig another one. Fonrouge and Crew went down, Mick and I stayed up. Saw Martin plodding up late around ten.

Friday: Martin arrived at 7 a.m., having bivouacked at the schrund. A great surprise: he was playing postman as well—mail had come. It was very pleasant to lie in the warmth of our bags, drinking tea and reading those pieces of paper which bridge such distant gaps. Martin was tired, so decided to stay down and extend the cave. Mick and I prussiked up in two hours to the high point. I quickly evaluated the problem and decided to go straight up the ridge. The gully and traverse looked wicked. A quick pitch up some slabs led to the first problem, the overhanging nose. There looked to be a reasonable crack for two-thirds of the way, then an indefinite right-traversing crack to some easier-looking ground. I cleared the ice from the start and moved right into aid climbing. Very pleasant A2 all the way. Then A3 on tied-off knife-blades across to the edge. There my real troubles started. The cracks ran out, and there was a stance fifteen feet above my head. I tried all possibilities, but couldn't reach it. I sent down for the bolt kit. Lurking in the bottom of the bag was a sky-hook, a small, hook-shaped piece of metal which can be attached to small protuberances in the rock. By attaching aid slings one can progress as long as there are nicks for the hook. A succession of moves of this type can be very committing: once you have moved up from a sky-hook, there is little chance of reversal. Above me there was a little nick. The hook fitted, a quick

move, and I was up. Mick jumared and I pushed on again. The
pitch looked easier but another illusion was at hand. After a short
overhang and a wall on good holds I arrived at another blank
section. Sky-hooks and Grade 6 free moves brought me out. The
mountain is certainly putting up a struggle. Late it was, so down to
the col. Thought it looked easier ahead.

Next day the three of us thought we would make a summit push.
Arrived at the high point around midday, Martin spent three
hours on the next 'easier-looking' pitch. Grade 6 again, similar to
what I had been doing the previous day. I joined him and tried to
push on. No go. I had dropped the bolts the previous day. It
looked like bolts. Top rings on a rurp—the smallest piton, about the
size of a postage-stamp. I tried, but bolts it would have to be.
Martin was on a bad belay. It was no place for far-out pushing. A
positive rebuff. A sudden wild wind and beating hail added to the
defeat. Down to the col again. Mick went down to pick up bolts;
Martin and I spent a wet night. It was still bad in the morning so
we retired back to base. We were now in a very good position, and
it only needed a settled spell like the last to enable us to make a
strong summit attempt.

Except for one excursion to the gendarmerie post, the weather kept
us in base camp for thirty-seven days.

'Sometimes one finds it difficult to retain a sense of perspective
about the ultimate objective. There are days when it seems climbing
has never existed and will never exist again. One also finds difficulty
in imagining the world outside—hence, the world is a few square
yards. There are no chains, but one seldom goes far from the
camp. Perhaps a brief look at the sky to confirm that it is really bad,
and a return to the present norm. It could be called infinite boredom.
It is, in a sense that one is being forced into a state that one would
not normally choose to exist in. But achievement of the end to which
this period is a means will make an eventual return to the outside
world more enjoyable.'

This was written during the middle of the period, at probably our
lowest point, when we were temporarily out of food.

It seemed amazing that we didn't bear any mental scars. On
self-examination I seemed to be O.K. As an introspective period it
was invaluable: I seemed to be able to slow right down but at the
same time to think very clearly. Time was barely noticeable in the

slow turn from night to day. When the cloud finally lifted we were fit and ready to go, except for Martin, who had strained a knee in a stupid camp game.

The long walk up to the ice-cave passed slowly and pleasantly. It was tremendous to contemplate action again. The summit seemed so close.

False optimism! This strange state of mind must have been occasioned by the sudden resurrection into a bright sunlit sky, away from the womb of the woods. The cave was gaping and looked very insecure. I arrived before the other two, stripped the tent and stuck the mattresses in the sun so we could enjoy a dry night.

Cooking started the next day at 4.30 a.m., and we were on our way by 8.00. At first the going was good and hard, but slowly it degenerated into a great slushy mess with the sun beating on our necks and heavy loads. It is irrational to get feelings about days going badly, but there seemed to be a strange listlessness in this one. The first fixed ropes looked all right, and Mick set off. We were belaying just in case. I reached and passed him, and there the first mishap occurred. Scraping about on the ropes I knocked a rock on Mick's head. At first it seemed serious, but a handful of snow congealed the bleeding and shakily he was able to follow on. Pete Crew was in a bit of a state, and obviously not going to be much use for any front work.

As I reached the top of the first steep section I could see it was going to be a hard, hard day. The fixed ropes ahead were buried and out of shape. The snow was wet and sometimes thigh-deep. The sun was hammering straight down with no wind to lighten the air. Ten hours later I reached the foot of the last pitch leading to the col. It had been a day of sheer will-power. Mick was impressed. Dizzy from his head he could only follow; Crew was only a porter. Defeating images were all around. The fixed ropes immediately ahead were worn right down to the core. Above, on the ridge, ropes which had been tightened down on our previous descent had been blown fifty feet out of true, stretched in weird shapes all over the place. I could see finish ahead.

Black clouds were rolling up from the Pacific as I climbed the last pitch to the col. To add to the good news the ice-cave had disappeared under six feet of snow. The guide-line we had left was snapped. No amount of digging could produce anything, and we had to scoop a hasty hole out for a bivouac before the full storm came in. There was no stove. It was a cold, huddled night with spindrift whipping through the entrance and soaking the sleeping-bags. The morning was windy and miserable. We fled like beaten soldiers from a lost battle, down into the Patagonian gloom.

Summer was over. Our equipment blown all over the mountain. The Torre seemed to have won.

Defeat is rarely pleasant. Sometimes it affords relief, but the relief is always temporary, suddenly eclipsed by the realization that you have failed. Self-analysis follows: you have turned back. Was the decision justifiable or was it made in a moment of hopelessness, when despair made the problems seem insuperable? The object of going onto a mountain is to climb it; to reach the end of your chosen route. It is very simple but many forget this. The story of Cerro Torre is the story of a defeat. We judge that we made the right decision, but we may be trying to cover up personal defects. The rights and wrongs, and our bitterness, were scattered by the Patagonian winds.

CHAPTER TEN

Yosemite

I'd heard so much, read so much, and obviously artificial climbing owed so much to the techniques developed in Yosemite Valley. It's situated in the Californian Sierras and holds what is probably the most concentrated selection of accessible granite climbing in the world. Ten minutes' walk from the car, one had the 3,000-foot walls of El Capitán to play with. Then there were well known names like Half Dome, Washington Column, Sentinel Rock, Mount Watkins, all giving visions of sun-warmed rock.

Climbers like Royal Robbins, Chuck Pratt, Tom Frost, Yvon Chouinard, Layton Kor, to name but a few, had completely revolutionized artificial climbing with the techniques discovered on these walls. The methods could not have been invented without new materials, and for this Yvon Chouinard was completely responsible. The traditional pitons in Europe were soft steel which moulded into the shape of the crack. Because of this they were difficult to take out, and usually malformed if this could be done. This had led to the practice of leaving all the pitons in place on artificial routes, so that only the first-ascent party experienced the real difficulty. Followers had a much lesser degree of hardship as they were moving up on fixed pitons. Then again, after several ascents these pins would often become dangerous as they rusted in the cracks.

Chouinard had produced a range of hard steel or chrome molybdinum pins which were designed to be used time and time again. The technique was to drive them just until they gripped, otherwise they would shatter the rock. On Yosemite ascents one took along what was known as a selection. This was a series of different sizes, between thirty and forty pitons catering for large right down to hairline cracks. But they were not left behind: the second man took them out as he came up, thus leaving the route clean, whereas on some of the major European first ascents climbers would carry up to two hundred pitons, most of which were left in place. Chouinard's pitons had a much greater range than the old, thus eliminating many bolts.

The techniques had come to Europe: Robbins's and Harlin's route on the Direct West Face of the Dru was a powerful example, and I had seen Layton Kor in very impressive style on the Eiger Direct. The material was becoming common over here, and I had used it frequently, but there was always a lurking wish to go to where it had originated—like a kind of climbing pilgrimage. But there didn't seem to be too much penance involved. Rumours were of long, hot, sunny days. Hardly any bad weather. The only difficulty other than straight technical climbing was hauling water on multi-day routes.

It had been a long winter in the snow. Making a ski film in Verbier, climbing the Argentière with Bonington, guiding on the Haute Route—the famous ski tour from Chamonix to Zermatt. It was great living—long hard days in all conditions from violent storm to snow-kissed sun but always with white all around. My dreams began to be of sea and rock, heat, and climbing without double boots, crampons, down jacket and big rucksacks.

'How do you fancy a trip to Yosemite?'

Bev Clark and I were sitting in the Vagabond at the end of the winter. I had to have a retake. At that moment I'd been thinking about more ski tours to make money. In a flash I was on the sunny granite.

'O.K. When do we go?'

'End of April. We'll take Annie and Jan and make it a family holiday.'

I knew he'd been there the previous year, so I accepted this arrangement mentally. There were still two weeks to go before we left in the middle of April. Thoroughly indifferent now to skiing, I packed a rucksack and drove down to the Calanques.

This is one of Europe's idyllic climbing areas. On the Mediterranean coast, between Marseilles and Cassis, there are a series of fjords called the Calanques. The cliffs get up to 500 feet on the edges of the inlets, and usually there are pebbly beaches at the end. Our favourite Calanque was En Vau. You leave the main road and drive for a few miles to the top of the cliffs, where you sleep out or use an open C.A.F. (French Alpine Club) hut. Water is the only problem: you have to bring big jerrycans in from Cassis. In the mornings there is a short scramble down to the beach, blue sea and white limestone. The days pass simply, climbing, skin-diving, swimming, sunbathing, drinking local wine, picnicking with fresh seafood, reading, talking. Time just drifts away. My white, always covered winter body became brown. Snow was as distant as the sea had been. Rock-climbing form came flowing back, and by the end of the week I was ready for even more sun and the delights of California.

We drove up from Los Angeles over some flat, dusty, uninteresting country, but slowly the Sierras came into view; then Yosemite. The first thing one sees on entering is El Cap. It looked more impressive than the pictures. Campsites are state-controlled and in good situations, but by no means private. The average American camper seems to travel in a closed-in truck, complete with air-conditioning, television and a full set of conveniences. We rigged a polythene sheet by the river and tried to forget about these things. One thing, it meant that you climbed as much as possible. We started off on lots of short climbs, of which the valley has many—really enjoyable routes.

Soon it was time to get into the artificial climbing, the East Face of Washington Column. Long, straight cracks for 1,500 feet. It took us a day and a half with a strange hanging bivouac in the middle, one leg on a tiny ledge and the other swinging in the slings. Nailing rhythm came towards the end. Difficulties weren't great, but the heat was impressive to one used to the Alps. Then straight on to the classic North West Face of Half Dome. After an abortive attempt when Bev fell down some slabs on the approach march, badly bruising his elbow, I spent several frustrated days looking for a partner, then teamed up for a successful ascent with Jim Logan from Boulder, Colorado. A really beautiful climb, comparable to the Dru, it made me wonder when I recalled the long lines of rusty nails of Europe.

An old friend, Rick Sylvester, had turned up in camp. Rick was a one-time climbing-school student who had by sheer hard work become a really good climber. His first artificial route in the valley was the Nose of El Capitán. It seemed a good idea to do a route together. From Half Dome I'd looked across the valley to another smooth, bald face which looked attractive. Logan told me it was the South Face of Mount Watkins, a Grade 6, first climbed by Chouinard, Pratt and Harding. Since then there had been only two ascents. I mentioned this to Rick.

'Why not?'

Next day we were off. The wall had a reputation for being hot. Laden with water, we crashed through scrub and feasting insects to the foot of the climb. It was supposed to be easy scrambling to a bivouac ledge at the start of the difficulties. Out of nowhere there appeared a strenuous little crack; mentally unprepared, I struggled to get up it. The night was hot, too hot to stay in sleeping-bags, but if you stayed outside a horde of mosquitoes would immediately start to devour you.

There was no urge in the dawn. There are some devious pendulums to reach the start of the main crack system. A pendulum is an exciting move, very common to Yosemite climbing. When one line of cracks runs out and there is blank wall before another can be reached, often this gap can be filled in by fixing a piton as high as possible, going down for some way hanging on the rope, then running back and forth to get up enough momentum to make a swing into the next crack system. Sometimes you end up horizontal with your starting-point but maybe about sixty feet away. If you happen to lose balance you come howling back at an incredible speed. Unlocking the key to Watkins' heart with a couple of these moves, we then hastened downwards to await a cooler day.

The sun roosted high and red in the blue for two more days. Rest and food and the beginnings of a breeze brought our keenness to an edge again. Evening of the second day saw us back at the bivouac. Morning after again very hot—temptation—there's a choice between up and down which is never easy. Why is the urge always down when the end-product of the up is so much better?

Awkward was the line into the heart of Mount Watkins—a pathway with many pitfalls for the wearying seeker. A tree that moved. A crack that knuckle-scraped and hammerblows back to front. Heat from the heavenly furnace, and the only way to pass the time was by climbing. This occupation led us to a huge ledge where, at last above the mosquitoes, we slept all night and well into the morning.

Onward was a thirsty trail with a crisis in the afternoon: a pendulum that wouldn't work. I ran for half an hour without success. Despair, then sudden light—looking up underneath the roof where my rope was anchored I could see a piton placement a few feet to the left. Up the rope, placement made, then the solution swing. But so much time had been consumed that it meant another not so comfortable bivouac.

The next day provided a highly original pitch. Nailing up a crack I suddenly reached a blank section. About thirty feet above was a tree. Standing swinging in aid slings, I had to try to lasso it—I knew I was in the West but I hadn't thought of a trick like this cropping up. After about an hour I wiggled the rope end back to me and set off jumaring up the tree. (Yosemite purists will do anything to avoid placing bolts.) Then nailing, nailing, but not quite enough. When darkness came we were separated by 150 feet of rope in a long, deep crack. We swung the night away, and then out to some fine climbing to finish. The last pitch is the hardest on the climb, a good way of keeping concentration from slipping. No Alpine summit, just a heap of brush and scrub, but the inner feelings of delight were just the same.

A long tedious descent to find a telegram: *Come back to Leysin. Much work to be done.* Chuck Pratt asked me to go on the West Face of El Cap. I thought seriously; for once work won. A day later I was back teaching beginners in the Leysin Quarry and beginning to have serious visions of a high face in Nepal.

One other significant event that year—I finally married my girl-friend Annie.

CHAPTER ELEVEN

Annapurna

During our climb on the Argentière in winter, Chris Bonington and I had talked of many projected trips to far away places. The more exotic the place the better it sounds, especially when you are sitting on a bivouac with spindrift pouring into your tent sack. Planning routes is a constant climbers' pastime. I'm not a good organizer so do not attach great importance to the talk until the letter comes which tells me that some effort is being made to get the thing off the ground.

One of the potential climbs that we had talked about was the South Face of Annapurna, in Nepal.

Nepal at the time was just opening up again to climbers after a closed period of seven years. Chris had quickly put in an application for permission, and two months after sitting dreaming on an Alpine winter ledge it seemed as if we had a positive objective to go for. I received the great news sitting amongst the Yosemite granite. It made for a happy day. What we were actually letting ourselves in for was very much an unknown thing for all of us.

Certainly the members of the team who had been previously to the Himalayas had a slightly better idea, but even to them it was pretty hazy. What we were actually contemplating was a new concept of Himalayan climbing. Previously it had been the lines of least resistance that had been taken; our dream was the hardest face on the mountain. All we had to go on was a blown-up photograph and some very sceptical opinions from people who had seen the face from a distance. But none of us had really been sold on other people's opinions of difficulty. There have been many times during my career when I would have been left sitting on the ground if I had listened to the views of other people.

112

As a peak, Annapurna will always have a place in the history of mountaineering. At 26,545 feet, it was the first of the great 8,000-metre peaks to be climbed. A strong French expedition led by Maurice Herzog attempted the North Face very late in the pre-monsoon season. They had been involved unsuccessfully in trying to find a way up Dhaulagiri, another 'eight-thousander', and had only turned to Annapurna after everything on the other front had failed. In the remarkable time of fifteen days Herzog and Louis Lachenal were placed in a position to go for the summit. Their successful ascent and disastrous descent make up one of the all-time adventure epics: both eventually got back to base in a severely frostbitten condition, but in 1950 there were no helicopters or light planes to whisk one back quickly to civilization. Almost total toe amputation and finger-shortening down to the first joint were the price they had to pay for Annapurna.

With our modern equipment, this type of price was not envisaged but we were going to peer into the unknown just as much as the French had done. The selected team was one of the strongest ever to come out of Britain. Most of us had climbed together at some time or other. It seemed like a good idea to have a collection of basic friends—at least we knew each others' likes, dislikes and idio-syncrasies. Little, trivial things are notorious for blowing up into major issues on Himalayan expeditions, and by knowing each others' habits we hoped to avoid this. An interesting aspect was that six of the eight lead climbers were more or less professionally committed to one or other aspect of climbing.

Chris Bonington was leader and Don Whillans his deputy—this looked like an interesting line up for leadership: Chris very much the mountain romantic, still an idealist when he leaves his contracts behind; Don, practical, without a romantic dream in his head. Mountains to him are a job of work. You get the job, are sent out to do it, so you do it as best you can. An incident on a subsequent expedition sums up his attitude for me. I had been reading Tolkien's *Lord of the Rings,* and Don had had a secret try at reading it. When I asked him for his thoughts on the subject, he gave a dis-missal glance and muttered, 'Fuckin' fairies.'

Three more members of the team have already appeared in this book: Martin Boysen, Mick Burke and Ian Clough. The other two climbers in the party were Nick Estcourt, a computer analyst with a good Alpine record, and Tom Frost, one of America's outstanding climbers and one of those responsible for the breakthrough in artificial climbing techniques. Tom was a Mormon—this seemed to be the only problem about his coming with the team. In varying degrees the rest of us were a pretty irreligious bunch, prone to breaking many commandments.

This then was the nucleus of our climbing team. We envisaged using a series of alternating pairs, with two out front fixing ropes being backed up by as many of the others as were fit, carrying loads.

On expeditions there are other members who are just as important as the main climbers. Without supplies and smooth-flowing logistics, things would quickly grind to a halt. For these tasks Chris had chosen two people. Mike Thompson, a personal friend with a capacity for administration, took over the very difficult task of organizing the expedition food. For the job of Base Camp Manager we had Kelvin Kent, a Gurkha signals officer—as we would be using Gurkha porters on the walk in this seemed a good idea.

There was also the very essential doctor. Climbing doctors with sufficient time to spare to go on expedition are a rare species. We were lucky to find Dave Lambert, a surgeon from Newcastle who was then at an in-between period in his career.

Another way in which we were to differ from the normal Himalayan expedition was in our use of Sherpas, or any other kind of porter, on the mountain. Sherpas were the traditional high-altitude carriers, but they lacked the necessary technical skills which moving loads on the Face would entail. We proposed to use them only until the beginning of the technical difficulties, so employed six.

The principles of the lightweight expedition had been used successfully by the Austrians Buhl, Diemberger, Wintersteller and Schmuck in their ascent of Broad Peak (26,414 feet) in the Karakoram range. They had carried all their own equipment from base upwards. But the technical difficulties encountered had been minimal and they had been able to push up fairly continuously, with altitude as their main problem. Our unknown wall, on the other hand, looked to have all the difficulties of something like the Eiger, with altitude and twice the length thrown in.

The preparation pushed ahead. Don, Christ and Ian worked full time on the organization. The Mount Everest Foundation

stepped in and gave us their full sponsorship—the first time this
had happened since the Kanchenjunga expedition of 1954, when the
third highest mountain had been successfully climbed. Departure
date was fixed for March; we would fly London—Delhi—Katmandu.

THE EXPEDITION

That winter I often had time to think about the expedition to come.
I was working on a ski film, and there were often periods of inactivity
during which I would try to evaluate my position. The question
which kept coming back and back was that of acclimatization to
altitude. There were four of us—Boysen, Estcourt, Burke and myself
—who had never been above Mont Blanc height (16,000 feet)
before. There had been examples in the past of brilliant Alpine
climbers failing miserably on high climbs. I felt I was ready for a
move to the bigger challenges but could also imagine the despair if I
found my years of experience suddenly invalidated by some physiological defect. I could put this out of my mind swooping around the
powder slopes, but always it crept back. There could be no solution
until I was actually on the mountain.

The other thing when departure becomes imminent is the thought
of physical injury. If you are employed in skiing it eventually becomes a physical effort to go out on the slopes. A broken leg is the
most common injury in this sport, and that would definitely mean
no Annapurna. Even though Mick Burke was in Verbier with me,
we stopped contemplating winter climbs, the risk of frostbite being
too great. It's a kind of limbo state that one gets into just before
departure for major projects. This, I knew, would be the biggest of
my climbing career so far.

As time moved on we also collected four new members—three
from Thames Television and one from I.T.N. They were John
Edwards (interviewer), John Lane (cameraman), John Soldini
(sound man) and Alan Hankinson. The idea was to send back film
and interviews for *News at Ten*. They were all climbing laymen,
and action footage would come from the climbers themselves
carrying hand-held cameras on the mountain.

The full story of the organization and chronological progress is
told in Chris Bonington's *Annapurna South Face* (Cassell, 1971). My

own part didn't really begin until we left London airport to the
snapping of cameras. The modern climber has come a long way
on a different road from his counterpart of a few years ago. Nowadays
one must seek money and consequent publicity through the popular
media of newspapers and television. We are still the seekers of
solitude and far away challenges, but we need the means to get
there. Taking a camera up a mountain does not disturb your solitude
or your thinking. What the public is seeing is the performance in
action; what they can't see is the inside of the mind, despite the
skilled interviewer trying to catch it in retrospect. There are so
many people who get a genuine enjoyment from watching people
do dangerous things. Often they know that these pursuits are beyond
them. But their interest is often one of the reasons for the adventurer
being able to go into action. Therefore, even on a straight give-and-
take level, it seems valid for expeditions like ours to be filmed and
written about.

I didn't have time to take in much atmosphere of eastern city life:
a few hours in Delhi and one night in Katmandu before taking the
inevitable DC3 to Pokhara—the last town before we started our
approach march. But already I was feeling the general change of
systems. The chaotic Customs, planes that never leave on time,
passengers sitting under the wings for shade—the cares of the
Western world dropping away. My thoughts concentrating already
on the task ahead: would I be ready for it? The question always
coming through.

Everyone met up on Pokhara airstrip, except for Whillans and
Mike Thompson—who were making a reconnaissance and would,
we hoped, already be in the surrounds of our potential base camp,
looking at the mountain for the first time—and Ian Clough, who
was escorting some overdue gear across India. I was told later we
looked like a bunch of freaks in search of a drug scene, with long
hair and tattered jeans. Well, it's not the appearance that counts—I
looked around my companions knowing the degree of hardship
they were capable of withstanding—physically and mentally. Also
I well knew my own capabilities. We decided we could afford to
laugh at critics of our appearance.

Outside Pokhara we stayed at a Gurkha pension-paying post
along with a British Army team, who were going to attempt to
repeat the original French route on the north side. Talks of traverses

and descent of each other's routes—climbers' imaginations are enormously fertile. I was still thinking of adapting to altitude.

Going through the gear I was impressed. The organisers had certainly done a lot of good work. The equipment was the best available. As I tried on my double boots, overboots, down suit and fully zipped windproofs, a brief picture flashed through my mind of Mallory and Irvine on Everest in 1928. What incredible feats they had performed on their primitive equipment!

The walk in was a light-hearted easy-going affair. Do what you want, walk how you want, alone or in company. Easy foothills, with glimpses of Modi Peak and Machapuchare coming through the clouds. Machapuchare is an incredible looking tooth of a peak. A party led by Lt. Col. J. O. M. ('Jimmy') Roberts, a retired British officer settled in Nepal, had come close to climbing it. Since then it had been off the permission and on the sacred list. I allowed myself a few dreams for later years as my eyes subconsciously mapped out lines. Meeting Don Whillans brought us out of our dream state: he had seen both the Face and a yeti. The Face seemed to frighten him less.

It was a year for a lot of spring snow. Much encouragement and bribery were needed to get our barefoot porters to the site of the old Machapuchare base camp, still a day short of where we wanted to situate ours. I'd like to see someone get me to walk barefoot in the snow for seven rupees (twenty-five pence) a day. Whillans and I moved up and established permanent base. Our job was to find a way through the initial glacier on the moraine. I seemed to be walking very well but staying in camp was another matter—a really bad dose of diarrhoea meant constant exits in the night, though at least no altitude-sickness symptoms were showing. But we were still only at around 14,500 feet.

The Face seemed to break down into distinct sectors: lower icefall and moraine; upper icefall; couloir leading to the ice ridge and séracs above; rock band and summit cliffs. None of these looked particularly easy, but in a fairly short time Don and I were established in Camp II at 17,500 feet, I'd had a view round the corner from the site, and it looked reasonably good at the least to the foot of the big couloir.

The camp site seemed good; we had dug for most of the day and produced a good platform snug against the rock wall. There was a gully to the right of us but no obvious avalanche debris. Don and I were sitting comfortably in our sleeping-bags just before dark, stove burning quietly, when there was a great rushing and everything went dark for a long time. It was obvious what was happening—a huge powder snow avalanche was passing. At least, we hoped it was passing. Huddled into the back of the Whillans box—a super-strong frame tent designed by Don—we could only sit and wait until it was finished or the box was swept away. Slowly the noise ceased, the rushing passed, the box was still there. It seemed that we had really chosen a good site. All that night the avalanches rushed past—it was rather like sleeping on a railway embankment with express trains coming through all the time.

In the morning everything was calm, uniformly white. The weather had already settled into a kind of predictable pattern: fine clear mornings with a storm coming in the early afternoon. Storms at altitude always mean snow. Consequently nearly every day new trails had to be broken between camps. We pushed on up into the bay beneath the large couloir leading to the ice ridge. Our plan that day was to get as high as possible and try to find a possible site for Camp III. There was nothing too technical in the gully itself. A traverse on slabby rock brought a spark of joy; then back to the ever upward plod. I could see where the avalanches of the night before had originated. There was an impressive line of ice flutings leading to our projected col, full of swept runnels. Also out to the right was a whole series of cornices and séracs. I flashed a cagy look at them: a little movement from that direction and the whole of our gully would be swept away. Soon these thoughts disappeared with the visibility. So engrossed were we with upward movement that the midday storm came on us by surprise. There didn't seem any reason however to turn back. We were warmly clothed. Three hours later we huddled on a snow step just beneath the col. Above the wind was beating desperately across the plateau. That was the time to go down. It was amazing how temperatures and storm violence could change within two thousand feet. Don had a pair of inadequate gloves and his hands had frozen up, so we didn't waste time but launched off down the gully in long slides. Soon we were back in the box, with the snowflakes just whirling gently around us. I was happy. Twenty thousand feet had been reached for the first time without too much effort. Realization also of the precautions one would have to take in a high-altitude storm—possible frostbite or exposure must never be too far away.

By mid-April Camp III was occupied, and work had started on the lower part of the ice ridge. All the climbers seemed to be acclimatizing well at this point except for Mick Burke, who had to go right down with a severe attack of haemorrhoids. This is a complaint that is often made fun of, but at high altitude it is anything but a joke. I had a bad attack while working between II and III, which, added to the problems of load-carrying and acclimatization, meant a great deal of straight suffering.

Here for the first time we ran up against some route-finding problems. There was the choice of the ridge proper, a gully leading up to what looked like a flat point high up on the ridge, or a large couloir which missed out the ridge completely. The latter would have been the perfect solution but unfortunately it was crowned by a huge sérac barrier. In fact it didn't avalanche much; but once would have been enough.

Chris and Tom started straight up the ice ridge, but were soon brought to a halt in the maze of unstable flutings. That only left the ice rib and gully. While the four of us—Don and I, Chris and Tom—were contemplating the start of this, the biggest avalanche I'd ever seen came swishing in huge powder gouts down the 8,000-foot face of the Fang, a 25,000-foot peak just to the left of Annapurna. A few days previously I'd been idly noting potential lines on the face. Shuddering slightly, I moved onto our route which, though the best of the three, was by no means completely safe. A huge cornice overhung the rib. Our risk-taking logic was that séracs move more often than cornices break; pretty tenuous reasoning, but the only form under the circumstances.

Various combinations of the four made good progress, up to just beneath the cornices. I was left with the job of breaking through onto our 'plateau'. The only trouble was that climbing on or around the overhangs was on completely unconsolidated sugary snow. It took a day to break through the first one, only to find a sharp ridge and one or two more. Two more days of slipping, sliding, concentration-soaked ploughing at the high-powered rate of fifty feet a day brought me out at last on a relatively level and sound part of the ridge. An obvious good spot for Camp IV. This was occupied by Martin Boysen and Nick Estcourt while we rested at Base.

I'd thought what I'd just done on the ridge difficult and dangerous, but it was nothing compared with what Boysen and Estcourt
had to tackle on the part of the ridge above. Overhanging unconsolidated ice. It was the hardest ice climbing ever done, and still
tackled at altitude. Overhanging ice is fine when one can put in
decent ice-pitons, but this they couldn't always do. Using devious
combinations of snow-stakes, 'dead men' (or snow-anchors) and
even rock-pitons, they took two days to come out of those overhangs.
The rest of the ridge was just ordinary hard going but very time-
consuming, and it wasn't until 3 May that Chris and I finished it off.

But progress shot forward again, and in four wild, stormbound
days Don and I were through the sérac barrier at the foot of the rock
band. There was a good site here for Camp V, but even supplying
it was going to be one hell of a job. A carry from Camp IV, up the
overhanging prussiks, along the horizontal horrors of the ice ridge
and up the never-ending icefields above was one of the most demanding tasks on the expedition.

Slowly little cracks began to appear in personal performances
and personal relations. Mick and Tom cracked the main difficulties
of the rock band, supported by Martin and Nick carrying between
Camps IV and V. Both teams were obviously tired, and Chris
proposed to shoot Don and me straight through to the front to
try to make some faster progress. At this time we were going that
much better than any other pair; neither of us had suffered any
real acclimatization problems. We were also still a long way from
the top, with possible monsoon time becoming closer. There was a
bitter radio conversation at the time, and acrimony for a day or
two, but eventually most people concerned realized it was the
right decision. Certainly the way things happened in the future
proved it to be correct.

It was a question of priorities. If every person had been going
equally well, then perhaps everyone would have reached the
summit, and 'fair play' would have been satisfied. As it was, Don and I
were the only people with the necessary strength to get through the
last few days of the expedition and still make a summit push—and
even then we were close to failure, as I wrote a few days after the climb.*

* The following account of the summit push appeared in *Annapurna
South Face*. (© Mount Everest Foundation 1971)

THE FINAL PUSH

I come back to the subjective above the col, doing what I'd been doing so often in the last few weeks. Moving slowly. Knee-deep now to be broken, a strange effort to lift one leg and place it in front of the other. It seemed so stupid. After all I'd been making the same motions for most of my life. I often wondered if my willpower was going to be strong enough. I'd spent many years training it to work in climbing situations. Yet trail-breaking at altitude is one of the hardest things to put up with. There's Don behind, but he can't help me. This kind of thing you have to go alone. Slowly as I look around, the doubt clears. The mind is a shattering brilliant firework display of incredible impressions battling with unforgettable memories. I'm not on a bed looking at a kaleidoscope of psychedelic colours and verging on the borders of insanity. I'm at 23,000 feet and sane, I hope—though many would question this. I've been asked so many times why I climb but in the ultimate analysis I often wonder if I know myself. Is this pleasure?

I am now at Camp V—lung-heaving tiredness—standing in a crevasse with spindrift pouring over me. There are three of us now, I lie making tea with Don and Martin inside the RAFMA tent. putting off the decision to go outside and erect a box. One thing seems good, the weather is still fine. This is one of the few days when there hasn't been a storm in the afternoon. The dying sun hangs fire over the Fang and out to the left we are beginning to level off high up on Machapuchare. It takes time to erect the box. When one isn't under the pressure of actual climbing lethargy soon sets in. But Don and I have clocked many hours in boxes to date and reckon them the most comfortable resthouses on the mountain. We do it and crawl in. The rest is routine. Morning has to be awaited. Martin has a lonely night in the RAFMA.

The morning comes and is not so fine. I ponder the day's programme over breakfast tea. The aim is an establishment of Camp VI. This means fairly heavy packs. Tent, stoves and camp-kits. Mick had been fairly vague about the possibilities of a good site. The Flat Iron had been his high point but he had been unable to reach the point where it rejoined the main cliff. From a distance it had looked like a possible, indeed the only, camp-site. The amount of work they had done on the Rock Band was impressive, I thought, as I pushed my jumars ever upwards. But oh, the traverses! Upward jumaring is at least rhythmic, but going sideways is a constant strain on the arms and legs and at least one-third of this section between V and projected VI was on traverses. Then suddenly I was at the end of the life-lines and also the good weather. Mick and Tom's high point was a rock about a hundred feet below the crest of the Flat Iron and about four hundred from the proposed camp-site. The cloud was swirling around bringing intermittent gusts of snowflakes. We three stood talking on the belay. Martin's feet had already gone numb. He was thinking of turning round and going back as I set off for the top of the Flat Iron. It was a long and tortuous pitch done in one run-out on one of our big ropes. Firstly knee-deep mushy snow, then hard ice to exit, with one miserable knife-blade for protection. The one thing to remember not to do on the Annapurna South Face is fall off. Then the big disappoint-ment. What had looked like a platform was a knife-edge ridge. So narrow that I broke through and nearly fell over the other side as I pulled up the last few feet. However, it looked as if we might manage something with a lot of work. Don started to come up the fixed line. Curiosity got the better of me and I ran out the rest of the rope on a self-belay to see what was round the corner. The rope ran out so I tied all my aid slings and runners together. It was just enough to see into a big gully. It looked good. There was certainly a way ahead for a few hundred feet. Don arrived and we went back to normal roped climbing. Yes, it was a good continuation line. I could see upwards for about five hundred feet, then it swung to the right. This was the important news. It made the fact that we didn't have a camp-site fall into the back of our minds. It had been a long day. We turned round in the gathering snowflakes leaving our loads at the crest of the Flat Iron and down the ropeway to Camp V.

Nick was there with Martin and we all sat in happy squalor in the box and ate the evening meal. But outside, the elements were anything but happy. The roof of the box began to sag as the spin-drift built up. Soon it had drifted half-way up the entrance. In choosing our site we had had the option of placing the box right under the lip of the bergschrund—which was the most sheltered, but this lip had looked as if it might drop off and there would have been no survival for anyone sleeping underneath—or placing it just outside where we were in the path of spindrift slides coming from the icefield above. We had opted for the latter and were now suffering the effects of our fear. Nick tried to make a break for his own tent which was only six feet away—he just got outside when we heard an agonized choke—'Christ, I'm suffocating.' Quick as a flash Don shouted, 'Get your head back in here, quick!' and an agonized distorted face appeared back in the tent. All was well. Nick had been having trouble with his breathing anyway and in gasping he had caught a lungful of spindrift. Finally everyone was in their sleeping-bags. No sooner done than Don and I had to get out and put our feet against the roof of the box and started a series of exhausting heaves to clear the snow from the roof. After our long day this was the finishing trick and we collapsed into comatose sleep.

Meanwhile next door the drama was not over. Around five in the morning I heard Martin and Nick get up and thought, they are keen: if they make breakfast then we can shoot up and establish Camp VI in good time. Then a brew came through our blocked-up door and I peered out to see two shaken faces and a scene of devastation. They had decided to sleep with their heads to the door because of avalanches. Some time during the night the pressure of snow had collapsed the back of the tent, smashing the rear frame and ridge pole. If they hadn't turned round? Nick was particularly shaken up and could hardly stop talking. Two suffocation experiences within a night at 23,000 feet. Trying things on one's will? There was no question of going upwards. The debris had to be straightened out. The box was almost completely covered. All the supplies were buried. It took a supreme effort to dig out the entrenching tool and start the excavation. But Nick and Martin still had to have a tent. The lightweight RAFMA for Camp VII was down at the col, so Nick and I went down to collect this plus food, while the other two moved the box and made a platform for the tent. The weather was still wild and windy but despite the setbacks I felt in a strange happiness state coming back up the ropes. I was moving fast and having no breathing troubles. Acclimatization was obviously working. I suddenly had time to think about life again. Often at high altitudes one's mind is working so hard that one cannot appreciate the surroundings fully. It all came rushing back. The things I wanted most. Big mountains, savage surroundings, difficult climbing, with body and mind completely in tune with the situation. I popped into the bergschrund in such a state to find a cheerful enough Don but

an unhappy Martin. He was feeling really low. To add to his tiredness from heavy load-carrying he had developed an infection from
the open cuts on his hands. I felt that when he made this decision
it would be the last time we would see him high on the mountain. I
think Martin knew it as well but it's the kind of thing one leaves
unspoken. Each to his own problems, hopes and despairs. One
less load in the morning and one more problem in establishing
Camp VI. The tent and box were much better sited under the lip
of the schrund so we slept a better sleep that night.

Even so, in the morning we still had to dig out the ropes and gas
cylinders again. Enough said about the fixed ropes between V and
VI. The clouds and snow set in around twelve. Don and I were
bewildered and lost at Nick and Tom's old high point. He thought
the situation bad enough to warrant digging-in as soon as possible.
The light was such that you couldn't recognize a flattish spot until
you were standing on it. He traversed to the ridge and started to
dig. I prussiked up to get the tent from the top of the Flat Iron.
Out of interest I started to clear a small platform. There didn't
seem to be too much ice. Out of the storm a cry from below:
'It's no bloody use here, I've struck hard ice.' I told him that I
thought we could get something in my position and he started up
towards me. Slowly a platform materialized. Nick gave a shout from
below and said he was leaving his load a few hundred feet beneath
us and couldn't go on any farther. I went down a few rope lengths
to pick up my rucksack, which I'd left at the point where Don had
been digging. On the way up I stopped to pick up Nick's load. Took
off my rucksack—a careless movement and that was the last I ever
saw it. It contained all my personal gear and food for Camp VI.

For a few minutes I knew total despair. I was going well—the
summit seemed possible. Now it looked as if I would have to go
right down to get reserve gear. Then the mental clouds cleared and
I began to rationalize. Perhaps if I went back to V I could borrow
two duvets, then bivouac in them until a sleeping-bag could be sent.
I could also talk the situation over with Chris. Don just looked at me:
he probably knew how I was feeling. He just suggested that I should
bivouac with his duvet and keep the stove going all night. This was
fine—maybe for one night but it would also have weakened me and
we also didn't have a radio to communicate my plight to the others
and Nick had disappeared before it happened, so I just said, 'See

you in the morning,' and turned round. The descent took only twenty minutes as I was so enraged with myself. I caught Nick up on the last rappel. He swung into Camp V expecting to find Chris and Ian but there was only silence and the swish of spindrift. More despair, we had no food. I—no equipment. Don was doing his foodless sentry duty above. It was late. It looked as if Chris and Ian had been unable to make it because of the storm. At least we had a radio. Perhaps we could get a little enlightenment. Even in this field we were having no luck. Atmospherics were terrible—I could barely make myself understood. After about five tries Kelvin at Camp III realized I needed a sleeping-bag. Selflessly he said he would send his up the mountain to Camp IV and someone else could take one up the mountain in the morning. It seemed a reasonable solution, but one that still left me at Camp V for a day. What about Don above? Then radio communications became slightly clearer. Chris and Ian had set out. Ian had dumped his too heavy load and set off downwards. Chris was still on his way. I got out and peered over the edge. There in falling light was Chris coming up the last rope. A good sight for my mind. He had a load of ropes. Scavenging the last of the existing Camp V food, we talked. It all seemed to fall into place. I was willing to set off in the morning to try and reach Don and push onwards. Chris offered me his sleeping-bag and we established by radio that someone would bring one up to Camp V to replace his. It all seemed so simple. Why had I ever had any problems? It was teamwork working to reach the ultimate object. Sleep wasn't so good that night. I slept in the rolled-up, frozen interior tent of a Whillans Box with all the spare down I could muster. Cold but bearable, and always the thought that I could go on instead of having to go down, defeated by a careless, silly move. Nick and I talked for a little. He reckoned he would have to have another rest day. Here was someone struggling hard with problems of altitude. I wondered how long it would be before the obvious tiredness would turn into complete exhaustion.

Morning again, and I set off to reach VI in a happy state of mind. At 11 a.m. I could see Don from the old Burke and Frost high point. It took me two more hours to reach him. The snow was in an atrocious state. Jumars couldn't help. If one leant back for a rest it incurred a great swing on the rope. The snow was deep, wet and sliding all the time from the ice beneath. One was so frustrated as to be reduced to cursing the surroundings. A futile gesture. I could talk to Don and he knew that I had some food and was willing me to get up quickly. Yet my slowness was as quick as one could move. I got there feeling a boredom that I'd seldom felt before. We talked and ate some porridge. That had been the only spare food at Camp V. Don had had a pensive night on cigars and snow-water. I was weary. Two rope lengths in the couloir was the total progress. Don reached the high point but still couldn't see round the elusive corner. Back to bed seemed to be the order of the day. That's where we went. Around 5.30 we felt the tugging of the fixed rope that went over the roof of the tent. Chris was on his way up but in a pretty tired state. He had had to dump his load of rope three hundred feet down and only our radioless state kept him coming up to VI. It was good to be in radio contact again, I had felt the lack of one when my rucksack had dropped. At first it had been a chore to use them and the jargon of Roger, Over, etcetera, had seemed artificial, but sitting in the specific loneliness of Camp VI it was a good feeling to communicate with others.

A word about Camp VI. The platform was not quite wide enough and the outside of the tent hung over the edge. That meant that we had to sleep crossways. The front door gave out onto the veranda, which was about three feet wide. On all three sides there were impressive drops. That night the wind started to blow seriously. Down below we had been protected from the full blast by the Annapurna–Fang ridge but now we were above that level, conditions began to get slightly rough. It would come in sharp gusts. During the lulls you would doze off thinking that it had at last stopped. At the crucial nod the whole tent would billow and shake. I often wondered what kept it on the ledge. There were only two tent-pegs and a fixed rope which ran over the roof. The only other thing that kept it down was the build up of spindrift on the back wall plus our body weight. At one time it got so violent that Don said, 'We'd better sleep with our boots on in case we have to get out of here fast.' This we did, and from that night onwards we always slept in a bebooted state.

Sleep that night consisted of a series of interrupted dozes and a stormy morning was conducive to staying in bed. However, we were so eager to see what lay round the corner in the gully that we decided to go out any way. There was nothing much to keep us in the tent.

Food level was porridge, mint cake and assorted synthetic drinks. Comfort level was a frozen sleeping-bag and a rime-filled tent. I dropped down for the rope that Chris had left while Don jumared up to the high point. As I reached him an hour later the surroundings were becoming impressive. The wind was blowing and though it hadn't yet started snowing, last night's fresh stuff was being blown hundreds of feet upwards. Every so often a patch of blue sky would appear, but it was quickly wiped out of vision by a grainy stinging white cloud. As I moved into the lead it started to snow again. The whole gully then began to move. It started with little avalanches coming down the centre. These were O.K. as I could climb out on the side. The snow started to get heavy as I reached a stance and I had just planted a piton when everything started to go. Powder snow avalanches were rushing over me and as I stuck my head up to breathe, the spindrift would whip into my mouth and nose. I just hung there waiting for a lull but none came so I fastened off the rope and slid down to find a similarly ice-encrusted Don. We didn't think the storm would last all day so decided to go back to the tent and see if it would clear a little. The snow was now coming down the gully like a raging highland torrent. It was a sobering thought. If it got very narrow then there could be no progress after a snowfall. At this time there was a snowfall every day. So we sat rather thoughtful in the tent pondering the problem. Slowly the day brightened and even the wind decided to give up for a bit. Early afternoon saw us back at the high point. There was still the odd small avalanche coming down but after the morning's effort we hardly noticed them. It was the same old style of climbing, a kind of swimming and sprawling motion in the loose snow. Don had had the brilliant idea of using an entrenching-tool in conjunction with the ice-axe. I now felt like a member of the Pioneer Corps doing a heavy penance as I lurched and slithered upwards. Trail breaking in that type of snow demands a special state of mind. You must shut off completely and only think of the next few feet. It is better to keep up a continuous rhythm, no matter how slow, than to stop and take frequent rests. After a rest it is that much harder to start again. Slowly and methodically I rounded the corner and there was the continuation. After about two hundred feet of ascending traverse the gully narrowed to a chimney which didn't look as if it held anything to stop us. That afternoon we reached the start of the chimney.

Back at the tent it was a lonely night. No one had made it up from below. We were down to a few handfuls of porridge but feeling happy at the day's work and the knowledge that the route continued at least a little farther. Radio time produced the day's news. The weather had been really atrocious below and no one had managed to get anywhere. Various parties had set out but all had been beaten back. There seemed to be a lot of surprise when I said we had made a lot of progress. Considering the conditions I think we were slightly surprised as well. That night wasn't too much different from the previous. Sudden violent gusts of wind seemed to like wandering around our tent. But like most mountain hazards the mind eventually begins to accept them as a normal part of the environment and after that happens the particular danger never quite seems so bad again. The most troublesome thing about the nights was the sleeping position. Being forced to sleep crossways I could never quite get my legs straight and Don was curled up in a cocoon in the corner. But night passed as it has done for many years. By this time we were getting really wound up and I had the stove going at the freezing hour of five. This could be a crucial day. Would the gully lead us out onto easy ground or were there some hidden major difficulties?

Going round the traverse into the gully was like entering a special kind of refrigerated hell. Don had never felt it so cold in the Himalayas and I had never experienced anything like it in the hardest Alpine winters. The weather still wasn't good and the wind was still whipping clouds of spindrift around. But at least the avalanches had stopped. On the way up to the high point we were stopping every few minutes with frozen hands and feet. The cramped hand position needed for moving jumars is not conducive to good blood circulation. I eventually reached the high point and waited for quite a time before Don came up. 'I had to take me boots off to warm me feet.' Enough said. I started off on the chimney. At this time we were badly short of rope and ironmongery. I had about three hundred feet of rope, four pegs and about six carabiners. The climbing was difficult; downward-sloping slabby rock covered with loose snow. Every strenuous move brought me gasping to a halt. One runner for a hundred and fifty feet. Then it eased to a steep snow gully and I swam my way to the end of the rope. The way ahead was blocked by a chockstone, but there still looked to be some distance to go before the gully ended. Don lung-heaved his way up. What to do? By this time we had been together so long that we hardly needed to speak about obvious decisions. We were both desperately eager to see how the gully ended. The whole way to the summit depended on this. So we just untied our belays and carried on climbing. This is where mutual confidence in ability shows. I was leading but Don was only about ten feet behind. One bad move and I would have taken us both to oblivion. Round a small rock rib up the gully a little farther—a difficult chockstone with slabby snowy holds. Spindrift and cloud whipping around. Cold hands and tired lungs. More straight snow gully. Out. We couldn't believe it. It was the best moment of the climb so far.

There we were sitting on an easy snowfield obviously well above the Rock Band and between glimpses of cloud we could see the east summit of Annapurna. The main summit was hidden but we knew from careful binocular study that there wasn't anything out- rageously difficult on the final section. If Camp VII could be set up in the vicinity of the top of the gully then we could make a reasonable try for the summit. Happily we turned and started to climb down as the usual afternoon storm came in. We didn't want the snow to fill in our steps so moved as quickly as possible. Light- headed elation soon gave way to grim concentration. Going back round the chockstone was breath-holding work. Soloing down steep mixed ground at 25,000 feet isn't the best way to enjoy a climbing holiday. But we reached the tent again so why should I complain too much?

Soon after we were back in the sleeping-bags, Chris arrived with more worrying news. We had lost the services of yet another high altitude climber. Even oxygen had not been able to get Nick up to Camp VI again and he set off for the lower camps completely exhausted leaving Chris to make a lonely journey to VI. He had brought us enough gear to fix-rope to the top of the gully but there was no tent for the projected Camp VII or any food. Sprawled dejectedly in the stormy sunset we talked it over. Chris said he would make yet another carry on the morrow to try and get us the tent and some food. It was the only way that a summit bid seemed possible at that time. I didn't think that such an effort should be made merely for Don's and my sake, so suggested that Chris join us in the summit bid by bringing his personal gear at the same time as the other things. His answer was an obvious yes and as he set off down the ropes the dejection began to fade away again. The odds were high against but everyone remaining was still giving everything they had. Teamwork was working at a maximum. Now there was nothing to do but wait for the Camp VII tent. We had enough rope to finish off the gully but it did not seem worth making two journeys so we decided to take a rest the next day and wait for Chris to come up with the necessary gear.

There isn't really such a thing as a rest day at 24,000 feet. The morning saw the usual rime-filled tent and frozen sleeping-bag. I tried to spin out making the porridge. We had been left a bar of chocolate and some nuts. These were added to the mixture to try and make something tasty. To our jaded palates it almost assumed the proportions of a treat. The sun didn't come around to Camp VI until around 9.0 a.m. A vague warmth began to creep into the tent but with it came the melting rime. Soon the inside was dripping. But we didn't really care too much. Talk was at a minimum as we had already discussed most of our hopes and plans. We knew that the morrow would be an important day. As the sun grew hotter and the inside started to dry our eyelids began to close. I lay in a half-sleep state feeling incredibly relaxed in the warmth. It must have been some kind of reaction from the long, cold, tense, cramped nights. Those few hours in the sun were more pleasant than all the nights I had previously spent at this spot. The afternoon clouds soon rolled up but we continued to lie and doze. There was nothing else to do except wait for the tug of Chris coming up the fixed rope. Late in the afternoon he fixed the last tired jumar stroke over the edge. Tiredness was all over his face. We had our tent and some food but he had been unable to carry his personal gear as well. A bitter disappointment for him. But Ian Clough was due to come up to V that day so they could at least make the second summit bid. A weary farewell left us to a change in menu—a mixed grill, with some nuts and chocolate left for the next day. Given good weather the summit seemed a possible two days away. Even the lack of stars in the sky couldn't curb our happiness at the chance to launch out fully again. Sleep was good.

I was once again up at five making the reviving drinks. Throats were raw from gasping in the thin cold air. During the night my whole mouth would dry up and I had to suck on a precious fruitgum to get the saliva working again. Consequently we had to get the first drink down before we would begin to think of talking other than in monosyllabic grunts. This particular morning there was nothing much to discuss. It was the day for establishing Camp VII. Once again it was cold with snapping spindrift-laden wind. The sun was two hours away from the gully when we started the upward jumar. I had thought previous mornings cold but this was the one that was way out ahead. Every few minutes saw us stopping to warm one extremity or another. For the first time my nose began to freeze and even with my face covered with a duvet hood plus balaclava I still had to stop and bury it in my gloved hands in order to regain some vestige of warmth. Don had his boots off and on but was still suffering. It took a long time to reach the end of our fixed ropes. By this time the weather had closed in completely. My immediate prospect was a three hundred foot run-out to the top of the gully. At first thought this didn't seem too bad as we had soloed it two days previously. But things were slightly different on this day. I had only gone fifty feet when I could barely see any more. Goggles were ripped off in a rage but then I found my eyelids freezing solid. I tried to clean my goggles and put them on again but they were totally useless by this time. There was no way of cleaning my eyelids. Dachstein mits were completely covered in snow and to take them off would have meant instant frostbite. Powder avalanches were sloughing down the gully and the swirling wind was blasting spindrift both up and from the sides. It was a nightmare climbing situation—yet the strange thing about it was that I never contemplated turning back. There was only one thought and that was to reach the end of the gully and pitch the tent for Camp VII. I had never thought I could get into as testing a situation as doing a hundred-and-fifty-foot run-out on hard ice in a storm on the Eiger with only an ice-peg and no axe or hammer but this seemed even more harrowing. It was twice as long and difficulties very similar. My eyes were so glued up and painful and I couldn't think of looking for a place to put a runner-peg. There was no contact with Don. The wind had drowned out shouted sounds after five feet. I fumbled onwards and only once did a brief thought break the terrible concentration. A flash of the possibilities of a fall. This was quickly cut dead. One doesn't even contemplate going for six hundred feet.

After I don't know how long the end was in sight. Ten feet to go when the rope went tight. I just had to ram in my axe and tie off the end as I was sure Don would interpret the pull as a signal to come up and I didn't want him to start jumaring with my body as an anchor. I just sat there numb and empty as I felt the movement begin on the rope. It was a total dream state and it could have been minutes or hours before Don arrived. It was in fact a long time. His appearance on the stance broke the dream state, face completely crusted with ice. Even then we didn't say anything about retreat. I fixed a peg, tied off the rope then we both turned and began to move upwards looking for a flattish spot to dig out for the tent. Don took over and we front-pointed into the clouds. Soon we reached some rocks and this was where Don had reckoned to place the camp. He started digging but each time the snow was taken off the surface, the entrenching-tool struck hard ice. Nothing doing there so he wandered upwards but the slope still continued steeply.

As I stood waiting I suddenly realized that the whole of the outside of my left hand had gone numb. I quickly stuck it under my armpit. Slowly it dawned on us that things were serious. Retreat and defeat were right there with us. Still our minds would hardly let the thoughts begin to flow. We were so keyed up for the upward push. Down we had to go. Even that was a struggle. Our tracks were completely wiped out and in the whiteout and wild storm it was hard to know which way to turn to reach the top of the gully. As we stumbled in the estimated direction there was an amazing ten-second break in the clouds and there it was about three hundred feet beneath us. Once there we still didn't want to give in and I tried to beat out a platform where the gully led out onto the icefield. Still no go. Every stroke met hard ice. Then it was suddenly inevitable and Don turned round, climbed down to the top of the fixed rope and started to abseil. Every foot we descended life seemed to get easier. Even though the storm was still at full blast it seemed relatively sheltered in the gully compared with the holocaust on the upper plateau. Retrospective analysis is interesting. We had been bewildered, lost, weary but still capable of making rational decisions.

Back at VI we found Chris and Ian. Shelter had been reached but the thought of four in the tent was something else again. Everyone was totally covered in ice. The spindrift had infiltrated the rucksucks and sleeping-bags were frozen and ready to become sodden. Somehow we packed in out of the storm. Ian was bent double in the far corner. Don and Chris facing each other with legs bent and intertwined. I was in an icy pool at the door. This meant I had to do most of the chores but it was relief to be occupied because sleeping was going to be difficult. Once I had to stagger out and clear the snow from the back of the tent. One good thing was that four bodies at least gave the tent extra ballast and there seemed little likelihood of it blowing away on this night. Discussion and tea-making was the solution to the night. It had been a defeat but already we were contemplating bouncing back for more. Chris and Ian reckoned they weren't going well enough to try for the summit. Their decision was to drop right down to Camp IV, leave us with the food they had brought up and then leave Mick and Tom, who were already at V, to support us while they in turn supported them. Don and I were to sit out the bad weather and then have another try at establishing VII.

The morning light flashed on our rime-coated bodies dozing in strange contorted positions. Chris and Ian eventually extricated themselves and left us alone once again with the wind and the swirling snow. There was no improvement in the weather. Sleep was about the only urge left in our bodies but the tent had to be cleared if we were going to do any surviving at all. Hours later we had all the surplus snow thrown out and the rime scraped from the bags. Our underclothes were still dry and with the stove burning constantly we fell into deep stupors. Thus passed the day. From the radio it turned out that nearly all activity had stopped on the mountain. There had been heavy snowfalls at all the camps. It looked like being a sit-out period. Most of the other really bad weather had passed reasonably quickly but this spell looked as if it had set in for a few days. Conversation came in spasms. Slight depression was beginning to set in again. If the snow got too heavy on the lower level there would be no carries. No carries meant no food and even at our present low consumption level we only had enough for two more days at the very most. When we did move it looked as if we would have to try and establish Camp VII then come down again for supplies before we could actually occupy it. The summit was once again beginning to fade into the vague future. We were alone with our sombre thoughts and the wind. Without the extra weight, being blown away again became a distinct possibility. The usual night passed. There was a gap where the entrance zip didn't quite close and each gust or jet of spindrift would seek out any exposed part of flesh. I slept with everything on, even overboots, and had the sleeping-bag tied right up with only a small breathing space. During the night the moisture from breathing would freeze round this hole and moustache and beard hairs would stick to it.

The new day was no better than the old. We passed it in the usual way. The only good news was the Mick and Tom had gone down to the dump at the end of the Ice Ridge to meet Chris, Ian and Dave Lambert, who had brought up loads of food and would try to make a carry the next day to alleviate our food situation. After the radio call I looked out. There wasn't so much wind activity. Some stars were actually visible and the Fang came into sight for the first time in three days. At least it looked as if we could try to establish the camp on the morrow. We were off by seven. Don left a few minutes before me as I was trying to organize the movie camera. It seemed like a good idea to take some film of the gully and also the establishment of VII so I stuck one cartridge in the camera and a spare in my pocket. The weather was by no means perfect. Spindrift and cloud were still making their presence felt. But compared to the other days in the gully it seemed relatively mild. Eleven o'clock saw us once again on the plateau. An exciting moment. In the clear spells we could see the summit of Annapurna at close quarters for the first time. I picked up the RAFMA and we had a short discussion. Don said, 'I think we should press on and find a camp-site as close to the final wall as possible.' I was in complete agreement but we were both obviously thinking of greater things.

Here's the way it looked. There was an icefield leading up to a sharp snow ridge which in turn led to a mixed face of around eight hundred feet. At the top of this face? Annapurna. Once again we just turned to movement without any more discussion. It didn't need telepathy to communicate our thoughts. The summit was a real possibility. The big question was the weather. There was no way we wanted to get into a situation similar to our previous attempt. True we could probably erect the tent on the ridge but it would be a bivouac without food, stoves or sleeping-bags. Certainly survival would have been O.K. but the weakening factor would have been enormous. Don led, I carried the tent and rope. Front-pointing up the ice slope the ridge was there. I just set the tent down on a plat-form and on we went. Time was pressing and there seemed no point in taking belays. Each moved upwards in his own special world. The climbing on the face was reasonably difficult. Little steep ice pitches combined with scattered rock moves. The mind was still working well. I got out the camera and shot off the first cartridge, Through the lens it looked sensational. A lone figure carving his way upwards towards the twin summit ridge cliffs, occasionally being blotted out by clouds of spindrift. I kept having trouble with my right crampon. It came off three times on the summit wall. But I was thinking clearly and stopped each time in contorted positions and fixed the straps. Due to this Don was about 100 feet ahead.

The wonderful thing was that there was no breathing trouble. I had imagined great lung-gasping effort at 26,000 feet but I was moving with no more difficulty than I'd experienced four thousand feet lower down. Likewise Don was having no such problems. He picked a beautiful line through towards the summit ridge. Then he disappeared over the edge and I was alone for a brief spell. The final fifty feet needed care. Big flat unsolid snowy rocks which had to be scraped clean. Over the ridge and suddenly it was calm. There was no wind on the north side. Long, relatively flat spaces led down into the cloud. Don was already fixing a rappel peg. We didn't speak. There was no elation. The mind was still too wound up to allow such feelings to enter. Besides the supreme concentration was needed to get down. The real problem was the actual summit. We were on a ridge. The snow peak to the left looked highest so Don plodded up the thirty feet or so to its top while I filmed the historic moment. Vague traces of what must have been army footprints showed beneath the snow. I, in turn, stood on the peak. The view was disappointing. Only the east summit was clear. I had looked forward to seeing Dhaulagiri on one side and right down to Base on the other but there was only a vast sea of grey cloud about a thousand feet beneath us. The greatest moment of both our climbing careers and there was only a kind of numbness. But we knew the elation would come when we unwound. Meanwhile, there was still the face to climb down. Fortunately I had carried up a hundred and fifty feet of rope in my pack so the hardest

section could be bypassed by abseiling. That was our summit
monument. A fixed rope. It seemed appropriate as it was the last
of fifteen thousand feet of such.

The down climb took all the concentration we had. Twice again
my crampon came off. Once on the summit wall and once on the
icefield leading down to the top of the gully. Going down the
fixed ropes the tensions started to wear away. It was turning into a
good late afternoon. Everything seemed beautiful. Inside and out.
I got back to Camp VI to find Don just about to tune in on the
radio. He handed it to me muttering, 'You've made all the bloody
communications till now, so you may as well make this one!'
A serious-sounding Chris came on, 'Chris calling Camp VI. Did
you manage to get out today?' I answered, 'Aye, we've just climbed
Annapurna.' Atmospherics were so bad that he asked me to repeat. I
was just about to do so when bedlam broke loose on the set. Base
Camp had been listening in and it had come across loud and clear.
Then Chris got the message and all the other camps and you could
almost feel the relief and happiness vibrating along the sound waves.

DOWN

Don and I eased out of the loneliness of Camp VI and began the
long descent. Across the endless traverses for the last time to Camp V,
and a happy re-meeting with Tom Frost and Mick Burke. They
were going upwards for their summit attempt. I really did not
envy them, and knew that secretly they probably envied us. It
seemed strange somehow not to be with Mick considering the climbing time we had spent together in last few years. Well, I knew how
he was feeling. A similar thing had happened to us in the Hörnli
hut before the Matterhorn in winter. The night before starting we
had to sit and watch the happy, successful Japanese team gorging
and laughing—their ascent finished and on the way back to Zermatt. Tense and nervous, it had strained us to be polite. Remember-
ing this I confined myself to describing the route, wished them luck
and kept on going. The rest of the way was uneventful but incredibly
hard going. The usual storm blew up, and we were very weary
when we slipped off the ice for the last time to meet a beer-clutching
television team, who had come to the foot of the icefall to meet us.

The next day I felt drained and lethargic. Re-adjustment was still going on violently in my mind. I just lay and looked into space. It was a wet stormy day at Base Camp, and I thought of Tom and Mick: there didn't seem too much chance. Most of the others in Base Camp had given up thinking about the mountain. Thoughts were of home, wives, families.

Meanwhile Mick and Tom had set out on their summit attempt. Unfortunately their physical powers were on the decline after many weeks on the mountain. Mick quit in the gully above Camp VI, and Tom on the plateau above. Desperately tired, they were now making their way back down the mountain.

Then at about noon Mike Thompson rushed weeping into the camp.

'It's Ian. He's dead, killed in an ice avalanche below Camp II.'

It took a few minutes before there was any reaction, everyone was so numbed and shocked.

There it was. We'd successfully tackled one of the world's hardest faces, people had been continuously active on the mountain for two months and then, on the last day—tragedy.

Relaxation can never be complete without everyone in off the mountain. Another friend had gone.

Mick and Tom had arrived back safely. We buried Ian at Base Camp. A simple grave, with the South Face of Annapurna as a headstone. Numb and pensive we left him there amongst the surroundings he had loved. Within a week the expedition was back in Katmandu.

Already Annapurna was in the past. Other things were in the air.

As well as climbing the mountain, we had brought another experiment to a successful conclusion. This was the making of a film. Although the official team never shot anything above Base Camp, their shooting there combined with the film shot on the mountain gave the necessary visual effect, much of the impact of the film was in the interviews with climbers coming and going from the Face. By skilful, intelligent and always unobtrusive questioning John Edwards succeeded in capturing the spirit of a climbing expedition as never before. This, from someone starting off with no previous knowledge of climbing, was impressive. On my next expedition I was to long for this type of approach.

CHAPTER TWELVE

Everest

I'd just established myself in the Shanker Hotel when the desk clerk handed me an envelope. Photographs, and a note from Jimmy Roberts: *'You're invited on next year's Everest Trip. Here's some pictures of the Face so you can get an idea of the line. I've fixed a meeting with the Japanese tomorrow at ten. Can you and Don be there?*

This was interesting. I knew all about the proposed 1971 International Himalayan Expedition. In fact the previous year I'd received a tentative invitation to join it from Chris Bonington, who was marked out as climbing leader. It had never really been confirmed by the leaders, Norman Dyhrenfurth and Jimmy Roberts. But now I suppose I had proved myself in the Himalayas, and the invitation became positive. This is a very valid way of thinking. The Annapurna team had taken a great gamble, with four of the eight main climbers untried in the Himalayas. It paid off well, but the Everest team seemed to have a lot of question marks in its composition.

This did not deter me from immediate acceptance. I suppose every climber dreams of a chance to go to Everest. Unfortunately, it's not just a case of picking up your bags and going. A trip to the highest costs much money. Also, permission to climb from the Nepalese Government is limited to one expedition per season—there are two seasons, pre-monsoon (March to June) and post-monsoon (September to November). The International Expedition had a permit for pre-monsoon 1971. Afterwards it was booked in advance till 1974, with no British party on the list. So it looked like my only immediate chance for Everest.

There was also the attraction of climbing another Himalayan face route. Repeating Everest by the British South Col route of 1953 would not have appealed to me too much, but Dyhrenfurth's plans were ambitious. Leader of the successful American Expedition of 1963, he had been impressed by the possibilities of a route on the South-West Face. His expedition had got two parties to the top by the ordinary route, but the *pièce de résistance* was Unsoeld and Hornbein's amazing traverse of the mountain, up the unclimbed West Ridge and down the normal route, the most outstanding feat in the Himalayas at the time. Face climbing was not then being considered too seriously, but with people pulling off tricks like the West Ridge, Dyhrenfurth was not day-dreaming in thinking tall. It was to be six years before Nepal opened up again to climbers. Mountaineering has been progressing. There were many keen young climbers, tried and tested on difficult ways in the Alps and the Andes, desperate to get a chance in the Himalayas.

The Japs obtained the first two cracks at Everest. Objective: Dyhrenfurth's dream, the South-West Face. Reconnaissance: post-monsoon 1969. Attempt: pre-monsoon 1970.

From April to June 1970 was an important period in Himalayan climbing. New horizons appeared attainable, thanks to the success of our expedition on Annapurna South Face and the Germans' on the Rupal Flank of Nanga Parbat. Fortunately for the proposed International Expedition, the Japanese were unsuccessful on Everest. They quit after reaching a height of 26,000 feet on the Face, complaining of stonefall and lack of camp-sites.

The morning after my invitation, we were going to pick their brains in the nicest possible manner. Thanks to a violent attack of dysentery, I never did make the conference, but Norman made sure we had first-hand knowledge by inviting along Naomi Uemura, who reached the summit by the ordinary route in 1970, and Konishi, leader of their Face team. Konishi I already knew as leader of the first Japanese team to make a winter ascent of the North Face of the Matterhorn; we'd met him in the Hörnli Hut prior to our ascent.

Sitting studying the photographs was a little disappointing. Compared with Annapurna, as a technical climbing proposition it didn't look as good. Except for the Yellow Band everything seemed easy-angled and slabby. But, being Everest, it would offer other difficulties besides the technical. Logistical problems would be enormous. On Annapurna we'd managed to do without oxygen, but the difficult part of the Everest face would start around the height of the Annapurna summit and oxygen would be essential, for both climbing and sleeping.

Flying out of Katmandu, I felt really pleased at having a chance to come back so quickly. I'd really taken a liking to the country and people. There was friendliness all around; urgency to do things didn't seem to exist. None of the hypertensions of the West. A relaxing atmosphere.

During the next eight months the expedition slowly became a distinct possibility. The great problem was money, and it wasn't until B.B.C. Television stepped in that we knew everything was on. I spent the time until departure skiing hard in the Alps to keep in shape.

There are various theories on the kind of condition one should be in when going to the Himalayas. Some favour going completely unfit and slowly getting in shape towards the end of the expedition; the only trouble with this kind of thinking is that those who pursue it rely for long periods on the ones who are fit initially. It's almost a parasitic feeling to have someone dogging your footsteps, knowing that you are going to get weaker while the person behind is getting stronger and is probably going to come through better in the end. Someone has to do it to ensure progress, otherwise everyone would be sitting at Base trying to outmanoeuvre each other in not breaking trail. I have always gone in good shape and lasted right through, doing a lot of leading, which is the most exhausting, on the mountain, but in the end have been right on the limit. Others play more cunning games.

The South-West Face, though the main objective, was not the only one. It was proposed that a party also try the West Ridge by a more direct route than that of the Americans, who had climbed a long way onto the upper part of the North Face. In the many expedition circulars, potential members were asked to state their preference of route. After many inclusions, exclusions and drop-outs, the party was eventually finalized just before estimated departure time. Final choice of route was to be made on the walk in, but choices were already pretty well established. For the Face there were Don Whillans and myself, John Evans, Gary Colliver and Dr Dave Peterson (U.S.A.); Leo Schlommer (Austria); Toni Hiebeler (Germany); and two Japanese, Uemura and Ito. My friend Konishi had to drop out. As a training climb he had made a twelve-day

winter ascent of the Walker Spur with Uemura and four others.
Uemura had suffered mild frostbite but was still able to come along.
Konishi however suffered so badly that he eventually had to have
several amputations. His place on Everest was taken by Reiso Ito,
who had performed well on the Japanese attempt of the previous
year.

The West Ridge team was: Wolfgang Axt (Austria); Harsh
Bahuguna (India); John Teigland and Odd Eliassen (Norway);
Michel and Yvette Vaucher (Switzerland); Carlo Mauri (Italy);
Dave Isles (U.S.A.); Pierre Mazeaud (France); and Dr Peter
Steele (Britain).

On paper it was a very strong expedition indeed. As well as the
climbers there were joint leaders Dyhrenfurth and Roberts; Murray
Sayle (*Sunday Times* reporter); Duane Bloom (oxygen expert); and
a complete B.B.C. unit—John Cleare and Jerzy Surdel (climbing
cameramen), Ian Stuart (low-level cameraman), Ian Howell and
Bill Kurban (sound men), Ned Kelly (producer) and Anthony
Thomas (director).

The International Circus was on its way. Everyone except Mazeaud and Whillans met up in Katmandu in mid-February. Ambitious
things were in the air. The B.B.C. were going to put sound and
camera on top of Everest. Their non-climbing sound man, Kurban,
talked of reaching the summit by the West Ridge. The climb already
seemed a *fait accompli*. Talking around, I was astounded at some of
the naive remarks. Too few people realized what they were up
against.

There was much to do at the Shanker Hotel. The gear had still
to be issued and repacked into porter loads. John Evans and Duane
Bloom with Harsh Bahuguna had escorted our ship-freighted equipment on the weary, trying journey across India. They arrived two
days after us. For the next week it was bedlam—boxes being broken
up, equipment issued, food packed. I was very impressed by the
industry and, not really liking this kind of work, I somehow always
managed to be superfluous. My days passed pleasantly in the
company of non-climbing friends, bicycling around Katmandu and
getting to know the east a little better. I reckoned my job would
really start on the mountain. In this assumption I was very
correct.

On the whole it was a happy atmosphere. New friendships

formed, old ones renewed. Each night before dinner, we'd have a meeting discussing the events and progress, with Norman carrying out impressive feats of non-stop translation in four languages. Usually most of the equipment goes in on the backs of Sherpas. We'd had six really good ones on Annapurna, and five were coming back on the Everest trip. Happy reunions—Don and I had formed a really good working relationship with our Sherpas. They will do a lot for people they respect. It was nice to see the old faces again.

We'd had a tremendous offer from an English light-aeroplane firm who were trying to sell a new model in Nepal. In return for publicity and advertising, they would fly as much of our gear as their schedule permitted into Lukla, an airstrip situated at 9,000 feet, just short of Namche Bazaar, the Sherpas' capital, and roughly five days from Base Camp. This would save us many porters on the approach march.

One day I flew in with the pilot and Murray Sayle to do some publicity photographs. What an airstrip! It's purely a grassy plateau on a hillside, with the strip sloping uphill for landing to help slow the plane down. You can't use the full extent either as there's a crashed Nepalese Army plane at the end. This plane is now derelict and useless, but the Nepalese Army had posted a soldier to Lukla to guard the military property. Could be one of the easiest jobs in the world.

Everest was in cloud as we flew in, but all around were hundreds of dazzling peaks. The urges were kicking strong, and I felt very like staying at Lukla and doing some training climbs. It seemed strange, as we flew back over the multi-day approach march, that what had taken an hour would soon take ten to eleven days.

The whole bizarre column left Katmandu on the 28th. Most impressive was Murray Sayle, in full Vietnamese combat outfit with an incredible rucksack on his back. I felt slightly guilty with my duvet jacket and book, but within a hundred yards two porters had been hired for the incredible Sayle sac. You often feel on approaches that you should carry a heavy sack to get fitter, but this is a fallacy. There's enough work to do on the mountain. The best thing is to take a light pack with essentials and wander along enjoying the scenery. I really enjoyed this walk. During the day for me was a time of solitude and composition of mind for the problems ahead. I'd walk alone, slowly shaking off the delights of civilization and getting completely tuned in once again to a mountain environment. In many ways it was much less mentally worrying than the previous year's approach. There I'd been wondering all the time. Would I acclimatize properly? Would I be able to go high at all? But with Annapurna as experience I knew that only illness or accident could stop me from giving a repeat performance on Everest.

A typical day on the approach march starts at 6 a.m. with tea and biscuits. Sun just coming up. Walk for about three hours in the morning cool to some grassy glade where the full breakfast table is set out on the ground. The Sherpa cooks dash off ahead in the morning to prepare this. Tea, fruit juice, biscuits, jam, cheese, peanut butter, bacon and eggs. Lie replete, resting and dreaming, till around midday when you set off for another few hours' walk. Into camp around 4 p.m.—afternoon tea and snacks, washing, bathing, reading, writing, talking, listening to music. Dinner at 7, usually at a huge long table in the open. Bed with a book. We take it pretty easy, giving everyone a chance to overcome illness and get some acclimatization.

Three days short of base we stopped in the meadows of Pheriche at 14,000 feet for a four-day training/acclimatization/rest/do-what-you-want camp. Whillans and Mazeaud had caught up by flying into Lukla, and the party was complete. Now the scenery had changed. No longer in the rolling foothills. Peaks surrounded us on all sides. The nights grew cold. Thoughts of Everest loomed large. The holiday atmosphere began to disappear. First Pheriche day I wandered up an 18,000-foot peak—this sounds high but was merely grass with a little scrambling near the top.

On the lower flanks of Taweche, an unclimbed 21,000-foot peak, there was a good-looking Scottish-type gully. I wandered up on the second day to try out my new German-made boots. They were clumsy and terrible; even with crampons on I felt uncomfortable. My mind went quickly into action. The B.B.C. had been equipped in Britain with a predominantly French double boot. A quick chat to Murray Sayle; he was amenable to a try-out. They fitted. A size 12 outer with my German inners was still much lighter than my normal 9½ in the other boot!

Peter Steele felt like climbing, so on the third day we tackled the

gully. Amazing Scottish type Grade 2 climbing at altitude. It
kept on going for a long time, and we got out around dark. One
more day's rest and it was time to move out again. There wasn't
too much activity around during these days. most people tending
to lie around and rest. Onward to Gorak Shep, one day out of Base.
John Evans and Harsh Bahuguna were sent ahead with a column
of Sherpas to pick out a good site. The day after, I wandered over
the flanks of Pumori and down to a great buzz of activity. This was
an informative wander. For the first time I saw the Khumbu
icefall—not too encouraging, just an even more confused jumble
of séracs and crevasses than I'd anticipated. Dyhrenfurth had
spoken of someone skiing through it on his Lhotse expedition.
That for sure wasn't going to happen. I also peered long and con-
templatively at the upper part of the Face. There did not seem to
be too much snow. A small inkling of size began to be felt when you
realized that what appeared to be small satellite peaks were in
fact Nuptse and Lhotse, 25,000 and 27,000 respectively, both giants
in their own right. But there was a great chunk of Everest rearing
above them.

That afternoon there was a meeting in the newly erected mess
tent. No time was wasted in getting down to business. The next day
Whillans, Uemura, Mauri and I would start work on the icefall.
At this stage both teams were working together; our routes were
the same until the eventual establishment of Camp II in the Western
Cwm. The management had appointed two 'co-ordinators' to
liaise with them on decisions. Hesitant to use the term 'party leader'
they had come to this rather weak substitute. The obvious climbing
leader of the South-West Face party was Don Whillans: his experience and powers of decision were much greater than anyone else's.
Somehow he was sidestepped and the position given to John Evans.
John is a really pleasant person but not hard enough to hand out
decisions to the type of person he had on his team.

Axt was co-ordinator of the West Ridge team. Also not a good
decision, in my view; I felt he was not popular with the Swiss and
French members. In any case climbing leadership is a very strange
and often much overrated thing. In places like icefalls, and in tasks
like getting Sherpa columns moving, it is necessary to have a strong,
competent command. But on the mountain itself things get less
easy to organize.

Many decisions are self-evident. No other climber is really going to tell me what to do in a certain situation, especially if he is at a low camp and I am high. Alternation of lead pairs is usually an obvious expedient, and once there the team makes its own decisions. Tackling the icefall, most decisions were made at the evening meeting. It was mostly a case of rotational volunteering, with Michel Vaucher working out the overall formula for the day's work. This is where more strict leadership could have been effective. Volunteering means that some do too much, others very little and some nothing at all.

The first day in the icefall was enjoyable. Some pleasant climbing, no big séracs and a little artificial pitch to take us out on a small plateau about a thousand feet from Base. Ahead and above was not so good-looking. Shaky icefalls and big crevasses with ever-present danger of avalanches from a nasty overhanging sérac field on the flanks of Everest West Shoulder.

Bahuguna said that the Indians had gone through it in around five days in 1965. It had taken the Japs about eight the previous year. Eventually it was to take us around three weeks. To make progress we had to make a camp half-way up, called 'Dump Camp'. While we were slowly struggling with the problems of the upper mess, Jimmy Roberts had his Sherpa battalions running smoothly up and down getting our supply train moving. Staying in Dump Camp was never a restful experience. There were always cracking and rumblings all night long. Immediately above was one of the most dangerous parts of the icefall, a 150-foot detached overhanging sérac under which we had to pass. Every conceivable way of avoiding this was tried, but in the end we were forced to admit it was the only way through. The Sherpas called it the Mane Wall, after the Tibetan prayer chant '*Om mane padme hum*'. When crossing they would throw rice as an appeasement to the gods, or chant prayers. I preferred to run. Running uphill at 19,000 feet is fairly exhausting, but it was preferable to the helpless, doomlike feeling one got when passing slowly under the sérac.

I had one terrible day with Uemura, trying to find a way out to the right of the Mane Wall and going in the Nuptse direction as the exit ice cliffs looked lower there. If Hieronymus Bosch had been given the opportunity to paint a nightmare climbing situation this would have been it. Everything was falling around us. Eventually we became so committed that upward progress seemed the only way out. This was close to the climbing impossible; that is, if one was still interested in living, as we were. Collapsing bridges, falling towers, rumblings, crackings beneath one's feet. Incredible tension in the mind, knowing that one little block is enough. We were blocked completely in the upward passage, but somehow forced out onto some of the fixed ropes on our original route. Completely wiped out mentally, we had eliminated just another variation.

Another day I was fixing ropes with Vaucher and two Sherpas in the upper icefall. Suddenly there was a great rumbling and cracking. Glancing quickly down, I could hardly take in what my eyes were seeing. It was only seconds. The whole icefield beneath moved. Séracs fell. Crevasses closed with a snap, shooting ice bridges up into the air. We were both speechless, thinking the same thoughts. If there had been anyone in the area there would have been a major accident. But later people started to appear. Everything seemed O.K. I talked to others at Dump Camp; bridges and ladders had been crushed completely, but the supply column had been beneath the disturbed part.

Working constantly in the icefall was trying on the nerves. You could take maximum safety precautions but there was always a high element of uncertainty as to what was going to happen. Things collapsed without warning, without reason. It was much more wearing than actual wall climbing because of these unpredictable happenings. But it was the way through. It had to go if we were to get to the Face.

The day of the final breakthrough gave some good climbing. We were four: Schlommer and I, Mauri and Uemura. After a series of deep, rubble-filled, shaky-bridged crevasses, we came up against the headwall. Three pitches of unnerving ice climbing saw us through. The last was artificial, using three-foot snow stakes hammered into the mushy ice. I led, enjoying climbing instead of hacking through rubble.

The icefall was done and after three weeks we were standing in the Western Cwm. It took a few more days to string this section with ropes and ladders. Camp I was established at the entrance to the Cwm.

Whillans now came into action again. He had been having a recurrence of his vertigo problem and had not done much in the icefall. Now he seemed keen to move and establish Camp II, so that we could get moving on the Face. Only one night was spent in Camp I. With Ito we were to find the way through the crevasses of the Cwm with Uemura and Mauri and four Sherpas were going to follow on later in the day. For the first time I saw the whole Face. Big it looked, but definitely not awe-inspiring. We had feared that the lower icefield would only be rock slabs, due to a very mild winter, but there seemed to be plenty of snow around.

The Cwm is a fantastic place, a flat valley enclosed by the biggest mountain walls in the world. On the left, Everest. Looking right, you have the flutings of Nuptse—running up towards Lhotse and blocked at the top by the South Col. Plodding up was not too exciting, but with such scenery it was a great experience.

Close in to the Everest side we found the remains of the old Japanese base, and here we established a temporary camp for two nights before shifting up to a better site which was really close to the foot of the Face.

There were still only a few of us up in the Cwm. Somehow or other the supplies were not getting up. Radio contact was not good, but occasionally we could get something. Everything was being stockpiled at Camp I. Some people wanted us to come down and give others a turn at the front—this in theory was fine and we were agreeable but the others didn't seem to turn up.

The first evening in Camp II, Mauri wandered off to see if he could find a water source in the moraine at the side of the glacier. He came back muttering something about a body lying on the moraine. We decided to investigate at once. The Sherpas were very superstitious, and the finding of a body in the camp surrounding might give them ideas about evil spirits and they could refuse to stay there.

Bahuguna worked it out that it could be someone either from one of the early Indian Expeditions or from the 1955 Lhotse team, both of which had a casualty on the Lhotse face. It looked like a Sherpa by the clothing. Finding a suitably large crevasse we dropped the skeleton in, returning slightly subdued to camp, wondering about the omens of our welcome to Advanced Base.

At this point the two parties split up and began to concentrate on their routes. Of our team there were Ito, Whillans and I in the camp. The day after establishment Ito and I went up to the Face bergschrund, climbed it by some dubious bridges, and fixed a couple of rope-lengths on the ice slope above. This was fairly easy, angled somewhere between 40 and 45°, but there seemed to be a lot of water ice around. Turning round in the evening sun we decided to come back the day after and try to push right up to the site of the old Japanese Camp III, under the shelter of a rock buttress at the end of the icefield.

We were four on the return: Uemura had returned to II and joined the previous team. The system of fixing the ropes was fairly simple. Before leaving camp we'd chop up the 1,000-foot drums of 9-mm. rope into 300-foot lengths. On the ice, the leader led out as much as he felt like then pulled up the slack and tied it off. The others jumared up bearing the loads. I led all day on the icefield. There were some bald pitches just after the schrund which necessitated using modern hammers and axes to avoid cutting steps, and here my run-outs were short. Higher up there was a good snow layer so I could fix a full rope-length at a time. It all depends how brave you're feeling on the day. Around mid-afternoon I pulled into the old camp-site. There was still a load of remaining equipment, ropes and bunches of pegs and two tent platforms—a great find as it would save us hacking out the slope. Ito and Uemura came up; Don quit just before the last long run-out and headed back for camp. Although the climbing was reasonably straightforward in a technical sense, it was a long demanding day both physically and mentally. We had been climbing between 21,500 and 23,000 feet for the first time on the expedition.

Sliding back down the ropes was something of a joke: you just fixed a safety carabiner and ran down the line. I was back in camp in around twenty minutes. There was a group of newcomers from Camp I. Feeling happy, I ran to welcome them and ran into the first taste of what was to come. Evans looking slightly uncomfortable, Schlommer saying nothing, Don gave it to me straight. 'They think we've been hogging the lead, Jimmy. Schlommer here thinks he should be out front.'

I couldn't believe it. Not a word about our day's effort. It had been a big push. Camp III could now be established and the real work on the Face begun. I didn't say much, just swore, threw down my pack and walked off to get some tea.

Don and I went back to our tents and pondered the problem. If

people were thinking more of fair shares than of climbing the Face—
what then? We had managed to overrule this type of thinking on
Annapurna. Here it could be a different thing. Being basically lazy,
we would always have been happy to step away from the front, but
it usually worked out that there was no one else around and as we
were theoretically there to climb the mountain we just kept plugging
away.

Decisions were to try to erect a box on the site of Camp III as
quickly as possible. The two Japanese wanted to go right down for a
rest; Don and I wanted to stay up to see this phase through. We
would stay until the box was erected and try to push some ropes
through towards Camp IV. After a rest day we set off with two
Sherpas in support; Evans and Schlommer were to come up later
with some loads.

Acclimatization was working well. I was up the ropes very quickly
and starting excavating the platform. Sherpas and Don soon followed. The second Sherpa couldn't make it and here Lapsang
nonchalantly wandered down, picked up his mate's load and brought
it up again. One person who was already going strongly.

Evans and Schlommer arrived later, and everyone took turns in
digging until, late in the afternoon, we had our site established.
The others left. Don and I stayed. It seemed very much like the
year before. Alone in a box and in front of the line.

During the next two days the weather was mediocre, but we
pushed another 1,000 feet of rope up the couloir towards Camp IV.
Above us we could see an old Japanese tent. Having run out of rope,
and feeling like a rest, we decided to make way for the two Japanese
who were on their way back up, and go down.

Camp II was pretty busy. I decided to go right down to Base,
reckoning on around three days' rest. A few hours right down, a
day's complete rest, and straight back through on the third day.
Don just wanted to relax in Camp II so I left straight away, not
knowing it would be nearly two weeks before I'd see him again.

In fine shape I rocketed down to Base Camp, exchanging greetings
with people whom I hadn't seen for two weeks or so. The general
mood seemed fine. Everyone was moving up. Reaching base, I
found only Jimmy Roberts, some B.B.C. and Jon Teigland in
occupation. The supplies were flowing well through the icefall;
Jimmy had his Sherpas working smoothly; there was a great

stockpile at Camp I. Once this was moved to Advance Base, both teams would be in strong positions.

Base is always a wonderful place after the high camps. Despite its inhospitable situation, all the necessary comforts were provided. Wandering in, I was met with a cup of tea and shown to a tent equipped with foam mattress and sleeping-bag. Meals were served in big mess tents. Already up above we had been living on a restricted diet; there was lots of good food on the expedition but somehow or other it never seemed to get to the right places at the right times.

The next day, the weather broke. Cloud was right down to Base and snow falling heavily. Above we could hear the wind snapping violently. It sounded like a big one, and I hoped everyone was safely in their tents.

Late in the afternoon Toni Hiebeler and Schlommer came into camp. I felt sorry for Toni. Great climber that he was, he had been consistantly hounded by illness and was having real acclimatization problems. He looked done in, and I didn't think he'd be going onto the Face at all. The appearance of Schlommer puzzled me. Despite his protestations, he had not taken a turn in front. Being a rescue expert he was to organize a winch from the bergschrund up to Camp III. A cable had been hauled up, but nothing had been done about fixing the winch. Now he was down for a rest. Ito and one of the Sherpas were in residence on the Face.

That night radio communications were difficult. We couldn't reach Camp II, and Camp I was coming in only in very distorted fashion. But all was not well. The odd disturbing phrase floated in: *Norman is missing . . . . Harsh is in trouble.* Call-ups were arranged every half-hour. Communications became so bad that we were forced to press buttons, three for affirmative, two for negative. Camp I could hear us but we couldn't understand them. Eventually we worked out that Norman had reached I and was all right, but we couldn't get anything positive on Harsh.

Next morning conditions were still the same, communications poor. Some time in mid-morning, it was at last established that Harsh was dead. No details were forthcoming. People at II seemed reluctant to acknowledge the fact. It was not until much later that I found out the story of that sad afternoon.

The West Ridge team had been having some difficulties on their route. To reach the Ridge proper from Camp II involved a long upward traverse on slopes which were in worse condition than they had been for the Americans in 1963. Progress had been slowish, mainly because of indecision as to what was the best route.

At first the Norwegians and Bahuguna had tried to climb directly up to the Ridge. This would have cut out an enormous amount of traversing if it had been successful, but they couldn't push it through.

Eventually Camp III West was situated at the end of the traverse but beneath the Ridge. An icefall was blocking the original line, so they had been forced to make a downhill detour and then climb up again before they could rejoin the proper traverse line.

While Axt and Bahuguna were working above Camp III West, Vaucher and Eliassen had straightened out the route. To avoid the downhill detour they had fixed a 400-foot-long horizontal traverse across the ice slope. This was secured at salient points by ice-screws and stakes. By taking this route, the way up to Camp III was short-ened by at least an hour. On the 17th Axt and Bahuguna were still working on the Ridge. They had decided to move Camp III a little higher to the Ridge proper. This was a fairly heavy task, and both climbers were getting tired when they started to descend, having established the new camp. In the late afternoon the weather was worsening fast. At Advanced Base there had been a slight alterca-tion that morning: the Vauchers, Mauri and Mazeaud complained to Dyhrenfurth that the West Ridge party weren't getting enough supplies up to Camp II. It had been noticeable that these four usually travelled light and Norman became unhappy with their complaints. Feeling that they should be carrying loads themselves, he decided to set off for Camp I to show an example.

He was on his way back with two oxygen cylinders when the storm really moved in. Struggling up the fresh snow in the Cwm he was amazed to hear cries for help from the Ridge. He was going very slowly, and this was when we got the message *Norman is missing*. But he pulled through all right. Meanwhile in camp the others could also hear the cries from the Ridge. It was late, the weather drastic, but a rescue team set out. The puzzling thing was that Axt was already back in camp.

I'll quote Axt's own words, as told to Dyhrenfurth, on why this should have come about.

'We were not roped together during the descent, there was no need, there were no difficulties at all. Since I knew Michel and Odd had placed fixed ropes on all the steeper sections, I left our climbing rope and my harness and carabiner at the new camp. At first Harsh went ahead. Around 2.00 p.m. the weather turned bad. Soon we were caught in a raging storm. When we reached the long rope traverse, I took over the lead and got across it hand over hand. It was very long and tiring as hell. At the far end I waited for Harsh to follow. Voice communication was impossible, the storm was much too strong. I waited for a long time, perhaps as much as an hour. My hands and feet lost all feeling. Then I saw Harsh, tied into the fixed rope with a harness and carabiner, groping his way round the last corner of the steep ice slope that separated us. He waved with one hand. Everything seemed O.K., no indication of any serious difficulties. I was really worried about frostbite so I went down. Just before I got to the camp I heard his screams and alerted everybody. I couldn't have gone back up as I was completely done in'.

[*When asked why he didn't stay with Bahuguna*]: 'I had no idea how bad things were with him, and besides what could I have done without a rope and carabiner? Harsh had taken his gear but I would have had to go back hand over hand over that long traverse! I simply didn't have enough strength in me for that, and my hands and feet felt like blocks of ice.'

No sooner had Axt arrived in Camp II and reported his companion's plight than a rescue team set out, comprising Vaucher and Eliassen, followed by Mazeaud, Whillans, Ang Pemba, Mauri and Steele. Whillans took the precaution of providing himself with a bundle of ski sticks to mark the way for their return. Thinking that it was merely a matter of rescuing a gripped climber, Cleare and Howell also set out, hoping to get some film. They soon returned however, for the light was fading fast and they were afraid of frostbite.

Vaucher and Eliassen found Bahuguna, still clipped to the rope about eighty feet away from easier ground, where he should have unclipped to pass an anchor point. He had lost a glove and a crampon. His hands were frozen, his face was coated with ice, and his protective clothing had been pulled up by his harness, exposing his body to the driving storm. He was in a poor state, suffering badly from exposure and clearly close to death.

By now the blizzard was blowing full force, rendering any movements nearly impossible. At first the two men tried to push the stricken climber along the remaining section of rope traverse, but the violent wind prevented this. They decided to lower Bahuguna off the anchor and then try to swing him across to easier ground. They had only lowered him a few feet when he turned upside-down.

At this point Don Whillans arrived on the scene. He lowered himself down the rope and righted the Indian and, after further lowering, tried to swing the casualty across the slope to the shelter of a crevasse that slanted down the side of them. Again it proved impossible, and Whillans found it difficult enough to keep his footing and avoid being swept backwards. The conditions were so bad that the climbers were barely able to move themselves, let alone rescue an injured man. With their hands frozen, barely able to tie knots or open carabiners, there was only one course open—to continue lowering the Indian in the hope that the rope would be long enough to reach the crevasse straight below. But the lowering rope proved too short, and Bahuguna was left suspended on the ice, about thirty-five feet above the shelter of the crevasse.

When I talked to Don afterwards, he said that it was obvious that Bahuguna was finished and he quickly realized that unless everyone got themselves off the mountain, the situation had the potential of a full-scale disaster.

'I'm sorry Harsh, old man. You've had it'.

Those were his last words. He was hard-pushed getting back across the slope as he'd cramponned across without an axe or rope. The descent in the dark was silent and tiring. It was a depressed and sad party that came back to camp.

Next morning Dyhrenfurth called a full scale inquiry, during which Axt came in for a lot of questioning. Many said that they should have been roped together. This is not necessarily true: in the Himalayas, on easy ground and on fixed ropes, most climbers go alone. Often there is great difference in pace. Whillans and I never climb roped together unless we're actually going up. Also, at no time did Bahuguna call to Axt for assistance.

Of course, moving unroped assumes climbers of strong equal ability, but to be a member of such an expedition should assume ability to cope with rope traverses on 40° slopes even when very tired. Axt is a very strong and experienced technical climber; Bahuguna unfortunately was not. Very experienced in traditional Himalayan climbing, he had been up to 28,000 feet on the South Col route, but this kind of climbing demands little technical ability. Vaucher had mentioned to me the Indian's unease on crampons, even on semi-steep stuff. He was also very tired, having worked longer above Camp I than anyone else.

Criticism has been thrown at the rescue party for leaving him while there was a glimmer of life, but Peter Steele as expedition doctor had said that even if they had got him down it was doubtful whether they could have done anything for him. Don also said that both his hands were completely wooden and frozen. In reality it was just another mountain accident, but during the days of storm that followed many people became depressed and unhappy about continuing.

At Base Camp life plodded on. I read and rested, thinking of the people above. Radio contact was always bad. Supply lines were cut. The icefall was impassable. No one could get from I to II. Those at Advance Base began to suffer from hunger. Camp I did not have enough supplies to keep themselves going. The high-altitude rations were being eaten.

In a slight lull I tried to lead a party of Sherpas through, hoping to stay at I myself. It was hopeless. Six hours of waist-deep struggling saw us to the site of the old Dump Camp. The others had tried to come down from I to meet us but were brought to a halt by a change in the route.

Two days later, with Schlommer and Teigland, I managed to force a way through and link up with Dave Peterson just beneath the final artificial wall. The way was open, the weather beginning to improve: action could recommence.

Leaving Base, I felt that this was the time. I knew I wouldn't be back down until the issue was decided one way or the other. General morale was terrible. Being ill is very seldom conducive to being happy. I'd very seldom seen such shattered specimens as had staggered into camp the night before—emaciated, sunken-eyed, with coughs that seemed to shake their whole being. I believed more were coming down. There is always a feeling of sadness and frustration to have something you really want taken from you by illness. For some it was obviously the end of Everest. It seemed almost criminal to be feeling so fit and good. The throw of the dice had favoured me again.

Schlommer, Teigland and I left to go up the icefall. My plan was to push straight through to Camp II. Knowing it was probably the last of the good food, I had overeaten at breakfast. At Dump Camp it all came up. Feeling lighter, I moved on up the ladders towards Camp I. Just beneath Camp I met the Vauchers, Peter Steele and Ian Howell. It was like a refugee group, Michel sunken with possible phlebitis. Peter and I had become friends during the approach, but he barely seemed to recognize me. Howell couldn't speak: it looked as if he would be lucky to get down the icefall. Only Yvette was bouncing; we embraced. I moved on to Camp I, and Murray Sayle and Dave Isles. Murray looked in good shape. If he'd suffered at all in his first stormy trip to 20,000 feet, he didn't seem to show it. Underlying his flabby figure, I began to see some of the toughness and dedication that made him such a good action journalist. He has a sense of humour, too. This may seem an unimportant thing to mention in connection with survival situations, but the ability to laugh at yourself, the situation and at or with others can really help detract from the obvious seriousness of the environment. He didn't think of going down, but wanted to continue in a couple of days up to Camp II. Quite impressed, I passed on into the Cwm. It was a day of strange meetings.

Wandering in a daze over the long flat section, I met the Sherpa funeral party bringing down Harsh's body. I could only salute and pass on. Near Camp II, a meeting with some more Sherpas. Happy smiling faces, handshakes. Feeling good, I moved on to II. Moving slowly over the rim I met the survivors. John Evans, considerate as ever, came down a hundred yards or so to take my pack. Norman, Mazeaud, Mauri, Peterson and last of all, Don, meandering out of his tent as if I'd only seen him the night before.

'How do, son.'

'How do, dad.'

Then I produced my ace. 'I've brought you a present.'

'Bloody presents, what good are they?'

I pulled a bottle of whisky out of my pack and his eyes lit up. I'd brought the one thing that could make him happy.

We lay in the tent and sipped and talked and I heard the full story about Harsh's death and began to get some lead-in to the political infighting that had been going on. Things didn't seem too happy. There was an undercurrent of tension in the air. Just before dinner, Peterson told us that Norman had decided against the idea of two routes. We were so weak that he was cancelling out an attempt on the South Col route, and all resources and Sherpas were to be concentrated on the Face.

This seemed reasonable thinking to me. Our reserves were low. Don reckoned we only had an outside chance of getting up the Face, even with a big supply build-up. Sitting in the mess tent, Norman announced his decision. Mazeaud and Mauri couldn't believe it. Their ambitions were to get to the top of Everest by the South Col route. They refused to join the South Face team, reasoning that they were not climbing well enough to take the lead and refusing to climb fixed ropes and carry loads. Ethically they tried to justify this by saying that they did not believe in fixed-rope climbing. But they knew as well as we did that the Face would not be climbed by traditional methods. There was a lot of unpleasantness in the air. During the discussion, Pemba Taki, one of the lead Sherpas and an Annapurna friend, leant over and whispered, 'Dougal sahib, the Sherpas want to go only on the Face.' That seemed to settle it.

In the morning Mazeaud and Mauri decided to go back to Base to consult with the Vauchers. Don and I were going onto the Face. 'We're staying up until it's decided one way or the other.' This was how I felt. From my Annapurna experience, I realized it would need some real forcing to produce anything. I was fresh and felt capable of doing a lot of leading, and Don was in remarkable shape considering what had happened and in comparison to the rest. He asked Schlommer to come up with us to III, but he said, 'No, I have a headache.' Don arrived livid back at the tent: the situation was rough and this was no time to follow a policy of one day's work then a few days' rest. 'I'm not going to fix ropes to within three feet of the summit and then let someone else come through and be the first on top.' Those were the Whillans sentiments.

'Fuck it, we're off anyway.'

Ito had just come down, after doing some good work. Ropes had been fixed to within striking distance of Camp IV. Moving out of camp was like walking into a new clear world. A heavy pack was on my shoulders but it felt as if I dropped two tons off my back.

The Sherpa morale was high, and we knew that as long as someone could effectively direct them from Camp II the necessary supplies would come up.

The next three weeks saw us pushing our policy of staying out in front to its conclusion. This time, it didn't bring success. It has been criticized wildly. But may I say one thing. Before criticizing, critics should have an exact grasp of the situation. Let's try and break it down piece by piece, to see who could have replaced us or perhaps done anything more.

There is the charge that we burned ourselves out by staying too high for too long. We had worked it out that by using oxygen continuously for sleeping, and eating well, we should be able to stay for long periods on the Face. There didn't seem any point in going to Camp II for rests, as it was above the level where one genuinely begins to recuperate. It was not like Annapurna where a visit to Base Camp at 14,000 feet did wonders, with green grass and sunshine, room to wander, excellent food. Advance Base was only slightly better than a camp on the wall, and certainly not better enough to merit the time lost in going down and getting back again. Base Camp was out of the question: to go down, have a rest and get back to the wall again would have consumed a week at least, and we did not have this kind of time to play with. Our oxygen policy worked. On the carry between III and IV, the Sherpas were working particularly well and were able to push up a lot of cylinders.

Our intention of eating well turned out somewhat differently. There was good food on the expedition, contrary to some expressed opinions—I had seen it down in Base Camp. Theoretically, to achieve maximum success, the people out front should receive the best food. This unfortunately didn't seem to work, and the higher one went the worse it became. The food that arrived had been consistently pilfered until only rubbish was left. The Sherpas are prepared to push themselves to the limit in carrying loads, but if they take a liking to some form of food they will consistently hoard it. Dave Peterson was in charge of supply sending from Camp II. We would radio down in desperation for something reasonable to eat, and he would send it off with the column. Very rarely did the goods reach us. My most vivid culinary memories of twenty-seven days on the Face are two tins of bacon and a chicken, which Pemba Taki got to us at Camp V by taking it under his personal supervision. Don probably survives in that type of situation better than I: usually overweight, he seems to be able to live like a hibernating animal, the physical demands nibbling away on his store of fat. I'm slightly different. Usually thin and very fit, I need food as a racing-car needs fuel. If I don't get it, I begin to lose a lot of weight which I can ill afford. It's fine to starve for a week or so, this doesn't do too much harm to my performance, but over the type of long, concentrated haul that we were contemplating it was to prove damaging. Though not damaging enough to have prevented a summit attempt if that had been possible.

I try to think back on the days spent climbing on the Face and try to recall a good pitch or even a memorable move. There's nothing that comes jumping out of memory. Even serious searching does not produce anything. Every major climb I had ever under-taken had its great moments of solution of difficult climbing. The South Face of Everest holds nothing like that. Annapurna had hauled out to the extreme the total skills of a team of incredibly skilled climbers, but Everest had nothing. Long, easy-angled ice slopes. Rock slabs somewhere around the Alpine 2 or 3 standard. I suppose the attraction is its being the highest. That's why I went, anyway. But technical skills are really not demanded to a high level: what *is* demanded is a lot of endurance and supremely smoothly operating logistics. We had the former but not the latter.

It had been said that we should have made room for other pairs.

Initially, we had done. Ito, Uemura and I set up Camp II; Ito plus a Sherpa had done at least half of the work between III and IV; Uemura led quite a bit between IV and V. But they were not consistent. The two Japanese seemed reluctant to climb together. Naomi would do a day's climbing and then rush off down the ropes to send his story and pictures back to Japan. Ito did not have the experience of Don and myself; he realized this, and eventually stayed up continually supporting us.

On the return to Katmandu, I was amazed to find that the Austrians Axt and Schlommer had been complaining about being denied a turn at the front. At the time I was prepared to let things ride and just hope it would naturally come to a halt. But the same stories continued to crop up, much distorted and exaggerated even by those who had not been on the expedition. I therefore felt I should describe the situation as Don and I saw it.

Axt was very shaken after the Bahuguna accident. He had pro-mised his wife that he would not go on the Face climbs. He came up again to Camp II with the declared purpose of taking advertising

pictures for some firms who had given us materials. Not knowing of
these intentions, hearing that he was in Camp II and knowing his
capability for work and lack of laziness, Don and I had sent a message by radio to ask him to come up and join Ito and us at Camp V,
so we could have four pushing on the final stages. The invitation
was declined.

Schlommer's case was somewhat different. One day we heard by
radio that he was at IV, ready to come up to V. At this point we
were desperately trying to stockpile V and with the amount of fit
Sherpas we were only just keeping ahead. Pemba Taki came up one
day and said that Schlommer was insisting on a Sherpa to carry his
personal gear to V; he had come up on oxygen from III to IV with
someone doing this for him. Don blew up and told Pemba that no
one was to carry Schlommer's equipment. We had carried a full
camp plus personal gear in the establishment of V. It was a waste of
a valuable load plus a passenger at V. The message was passed on and
we didn't see Schlommer again. The next news we heard was that
he was in Katmandu, complaining to the Press about being denied
his turn at the front and that everything was an Anglo-Saxon
conspiracy to prevent him getting to the top.

I suppose our thinking could be considered too harsh. There are
and have been many people who think that Sherpas should carry
all personal gear as well as loads. We had proved on Annapurna
that this is an impractical idea. In my opinion every climber on a
Himalayan face must function to the maximum of his ability.
When material and manpower are short, there is just no place for a
person to come unladen up the mountain.

A DAY'S WORK

Early morning in Camp V. I woke sucking still on the now empty
oxygen tube. The mask had been condensing badly in the night. It
was a choice between a wet then frozen face or a very dry throat,
and I opted for the latter. This means taking off the mask and just
sticking the tube into your mouth. There was no such thing as an
undisturbed night's sleep. Somewhere around 2.00 to 3.00 a.m.
the shared cylinder always ran out. A frozen-fingered half-hour
to change it. We could each have taken one and continued straight
through, but we were using up the left-over oxygen from the day's

work. Every breath counted, the way the supplies were getting slower and slower.

Pushing my head out of the hood cracks quantities of rime. The rest of the bag is encased in a thin coating of ice. This will melt and become sodden when the stove starts. The stove is lit. Slowly we come round. No hurried movement. The brain seems slowed down. Coughing that seems to turn your lungs inside out. Finally the first drink. Now different thoughts begin to filter the brain. Not just ideas of survival, but plans to continue up this mountain. There's no breakfast food, as usual. A few nuts, piece of chocolate, some more tea or coffee, not very much to drive the human engine for a day above 26,000 feet. Getting ready takes a long time. Oxygen masks have to be unfrozen. Cold-fingered attachment of cylinders. We're pushing for a site for Camp VI.

Already we've fixed a few hundred feet of rope. We want to try to get a tent at the end of the rightward-starting snowfield beneath the rock band. At the right edge of the band there's a promising-looking chimney leading through to a couloir going up to the ridge between the south and main summits: 1,500 feet maybe. Technically it looks steeper and harder than what we have done on the Face. But that still makes it barely very hard. Jumaring up the ropes, I feel tired. Very tired, tireder than any other time on the trip. I try to think about it. The previous day I was going well. For three hours I struggle up. There comes a sudden stop. I seem to be finished. Well, I think, so this is how it finally gets you. I look down at my mask and crunch the diaphragm; crackling of ice. A few different thoughts seep slowly into my head. Off with the cylinders. Relief at the solution and anger at my stupidity. The gauge is full. I've been dragging along sucking ordinary air through my mask with no oxygen coming from the cylinder. This is much more demanding than just breathing ordinary air, which is demanding enough. The diaphragm is by now completely frozen. I'm ready to start leading out rope again. Dumping my mask and cylinder I set off, breathing normally. After my experience of the last few hours, it seems like sea level. I move well and quickly; altitude around 27,000 feet.

Experimenting with the use and non-use of oxygen was something I worked at. Between 26,000 and 27,000 feet I found that one could put down the oxygen for periods and climb reasonably well, leading or following without loads. But if one was doing heavy work, carrying

ropes or other gear, the oxygen really made a difference. Also, one
had to watch any extreme effort without oxygen as it seems to take
a long time to recover from it. If, in fact, one recovers from it at all.
The climbing finishes at dusk, still short of the projected camp-site.

DEFEAT

Things were going well above. Some more rope and oxygen and
Camp VI could be established. But the loading up from IV or V
was getting slower and slower. We were having a day in the box;
high winds and whipping spindrift. Morale was sinking again.
Uemura appears again with two Sherpas with heavy loads. It's
amazing how moods change. One minute, gentle sinking depression
and the next a sudden rushing optimism. The next day we had
enough manpower to establish VI.

It was a fine day. Ito and Uemura moved ahead with the two
Sherpas. Don and I didn't hurry. A methodical packing of our
equipment. We would be occupying the tent at Camp VI. Naomi
was going well, but the others were showing obvious tiredness
signs. We reached the camp-site; slowly people filtered in. All
except one Sherpa who had been going very slowly; it didn't seem
as if he would make it. Naomi rushed down, promising to check
what had happened. We needed his load badly. My oxygen diaphragm had iced up again. Don suggested I should go look for the
load, while he worked on the camp-site. Foolishly I accepted—*his*
set was working. Down I went once again without oxygen. Meanwhile Naomi had picked up the load and had started back again—a
good gesture. We met around 400 feet down and I immediately
started back up with the gear.

The camp-site was a miserable place. One tent, stuck in a kind of
grotto. Proof probably against a storm, but draughty, with no sun,
and very cold. Taking stock, we didn't have very much. About 400
feet of rope, two full oxygen cylinders and two half-used ones. No
real food to speak of. The night was long and cough-racked. The
next day's plan was to fix the rope as high as we could in the gully.
There was a snow slope running out round the edge of a rocky
corner to the right. It looked easier. Don soloed round the corner
while I was bringing up the ropes, and made the amazing discovery
that, by walking round, he was on easy ground leading to the south

summit. A tough decision. Reckoning it out, we concluded that we were still committed to the South Face. There didn't seem any point somehow in sneaking onto the normal route, after having put so much into climbing the Face. If that had been our intention we would have joined Mazeaud, Mauri, and the Vauchers one month ago. Coming back round the corner, we moved into the gully: straightforward climbing with lots of powder snow. The rope didn't last long or go very far up the gully. There was still a long way to go. We reckoned our high point to be around 27,500 feet. Don came sliding down the rope.

'I think we've had it, lad.'

Pretty much the same kind of thinking had been going on in my head. We were out of rope and oxygen and food. It looked as if we would need another camp at the top of the chimney. Down at Camp V there was only Ito and the Sherpa Par Temba—Uemura had gone back to Camp II. On a carry from V to VI they could barely carry enough to keep us supplied for a day, and there was no way they were going to be able to keep going for day after day. A good load for one climber was one oxygen cylinder for himself plus a spare for us. This gave a loading of thirty pounds, very heavy at 27,500 ft. Normally one only used half a cylinder between V and VI. This in a theoretical carry would give enough oxygen and rope for one day's climbing for the two of us. To climb the chimney, establish a camp and make a reasonable summit push we reckoned on six or seven more days, which would have meant at least a steady carry by four people from V to stockpile enough supplies. It was all over; descent was on for the next morning. Going down was uneventful. Don rocketed down at high speed, sucking great gulps of malt whisky. Reaching Camp II more slowly, I found out that my wife, Anne, was in Base Camp, suffering from cerebral oedema. I didn't stop for long, grabbed some drinks and bacon and reached Base Camp in a mere three hours, to find her sucking oxygen but recovering fast. A few days later we were both in Katmandu, thin but completely recovered.

Controversy was raging thick and fast. I'd had enough, and fled to the Greek islands to recover some of my lost weight and compose my whirling mind.

Reflection convinced me that we'd done the maximum to achieve success. It had not been enough, but that was reason enough for wanting to go back.

Index